The Instant
BEAN

The Instant
BEAN

SALLY AND MARTIN STONE

BANTAM BOOKS
New York   Toronto   London   Sydney   Auckland

THE INSTANT BEAN
A Bantam Book / June 1996

Book design by Donna Sinisgalli

Library of Congress Cataloging-in-Publication Data
Stone, Sally.
The instant bean / Sally and Martin Stone.
p.   cm.
Includes index.
ISBN 0–553–37455–9
1. Cookery (Beans)   I. Stone, Martin, 1928–   . II. Title.
TX803.B4S762   1996
641.6'565—dc20   95-44067
                              CIP

Published simultaneously in the United States and Canada

Bantam Books are published by Bantam Books, a division of Bantam Doubleday Dell Publishing Group, Inc. Its trademark, consisting of the words "Bantam Books" and the portrayal of a rooster, is Registered in U.S. Patent and Trademark Office and in other countries. Marca Registrada. Bantam Books, 1540 Broadway, New York, New York 10036.

PRINTED IN THE UNITED STATES OF AMERICA
FFG   10 9 8 7 6 5 4 3 2 1

CONTENTS

ACKNOWLEDGMENTS

People who love food seem to be very generous with their time, energy, and knowledge. We are especially indebted to Phil Teverow—vice president of product development at Bri-Al, L.P., a company that distributes, among other specialty foods, many different varieties of dried beans—for his descriptions and background information about many of the beans that appear in the "Meet the Beans" chapter of this book. When you need help, always ask a busy man.

We would also like to thank Patti Bazel Geil, whose 1994 research study in collaboration with Dr. James W. Anderson of the Endocrine-Metabolic Section, VA Medical Center, Lexington, KY, proved canned beans (our favorites) the winner at lowering cholesterol over soybean protein (the media's darling).

The idea for *The Instant Bean* seemed to evolve naturally from our first bean cookbook, *The Brilliant Bean*. But it was really our editor, Fran McCullough, who made it happen. Her enthusiasm about the project turned some musings over lunch one day into the reality you now hold in your hands.

INTRODUCTION

The recipes in this book take only 5 to 30 minutes to prepare. Yet as easygoing as they are, they have a depth of flavor, are as delicious, inventive, elegant, sophisticated, economical, and nutritious as bean dishes that spend hours in the pot.

Some of these recipes never even get to the stove—their ingredients are merely assembled. Our object is to get you to the table as fast as we possibly can.

Our recipes are often inspirations, utilizing foods that are near at hand. They are home cooking, not restaurant haute cuisine. However, they always rely on the best ingredients available, simply and speedily prepared. Stock your kitchen cupboards with the best quality you can afford, and you'll be ready to fly through the prep time.

HOW TO TRANSFORM SLOWPOKE BEANS INTO FAST FOOD

There are several ways to speed up the process—using canned beans, your own presoaked frozen beans, and quick-soak methods. When you're ready to cook, a pressure cooker can speed things up considerably.

CANNED BEANS

Canned beans are a wonderful convenience, presoaked and precooked. The downside is that sometimes their texture is mushy from overcooking and over-processing. But recently food manufacturers have become more careful in the cooking and canning processes, and now many brands come much closer to the quality of labor-intensive home-cooked beans. Keep looking until you find a brand you're happy with. We like the Goya brand because of the variety and the care the company takes *not* to overcook the beans. They can be found in many parts of the country in their own special section of the supermarket and in Hispanic food stores. Progresso is another good brand, although the variety of beans is not nearly as extensive as Goya's. Often Progresso beans can be found in the Italian section of markets or with other canned beans and vegetables. Incidentally, the texture of chickpeas and black beans suffers least in the canning process—as do any of the smaller bean varieties. Organically grown beans can be found canned in health food stores. The Eden brand offers an interesting selection, adzuki among them. Always drain and thoroughly rinse canned beans before adding them to a recipe. The viscous liquid contains excess salt and sugars—especially sugars that the body cannot digest. It is these sugars (called *oligosaccharides;* see the end of this Introduction) that can cause flatulence, i.e., gas. Rinse them away, and you wash away most of the problems associated with beans, canned *or* homemade.

It is not necessary to recook canned beans since they're already cooked. Just heat them—if a recipe calls for it. And even in the short amount of time it takes to heat them through, canned beans readily absorb flavors from other ingredients in a dish because their skins are completely permeable.

COOK AND FREEZE

With dried beans (the most economical beans you can buy) it's the soaking and long simmering that take time and forethought. Once these two chores are done, home-cooked beans are ready to eat, ready to use just like canned beans.

Why bother with dried beans at all? Because they are more economical than canned beans (which are pretty economical themselves) and because you might want to use unusual beans that are not readily available in cans or frozen. So if you're a purist and like to cook your own dried beans rather than use canned, another way to turn beans into *faster* food is to soak a large quantity, cook them thoroughly in plain tap water—without seasoning—then drain, rinse, and freeze them in recipe-portioned containers (2-cup sizes are the most convenient) to use whenever the urge strikes. These frozen presoaked and cooked beans keep for months in the freezer. Frozen beans can be added to soups right from the freezer (just add a few minutes to the cooking time to be sure they are heated through). Or blanch them in boiling water for a minute or two until they separate; then drain well and use as you would canned beans, again adjusting the cooking time. Or empty a container of frozen beans into a colander and run under hot tap water for 30 seconds to 1 minute (or more, depending on the size of the block of beans) to separate and thaw the beans enough to use in most recipes. Drain well before using. Allow extra time for heating through. Frozen beans can be thawed in the refrigerator overnight or left at room temperature for an hour or two.

The Less-than-Overnight Soak. Most recipes for dried beans tell you to soak them overnight. This is merely for convenience. They won't absorb any more moisture from the long soaking than they would from a 4-hour soak (as much as even the oldest, most defiant beans ever need, except for favas or soybeans, whose thick skins require about 12 hours of soaking to revitalize).

The Mexican Way or *No-Soak Method.* Most Mexican cooks never soak beans; they just cook dried beans very slowly, covered, for $1^1/_2$ to 4 hours, depending on the variety of the bean.

Bring water to cover the beans by 1 inch to a boil, then reduce the heat to a bare simmer and cook, covered, adding at least 30 to 60 minutes to the cooking times suggested in the chart in this chapter, until tender. Check every once in a

---

QUICK SOAKING METHODS FOR DRIED BEANS

When you don't have time for a soak of 2 to 4 hours or have not thought ahead, use one of these faster methods. The loss of nutrients because of higher-temperature quick soaking is negligible—just eat an extra forkful or two.

METHOD 1: 1 HOUR
1. Place the washed and picked-over beans in a large saucepan and cover with 2 inches of fresh unsalted water.
2. Bring to a boil and boil for 2 minutes.
3. Remove the pan from the heat and soak, covered, for 1 hour.
4. Discard the soaking water, rinse the beans, and they are ready to cook.

METHOD 2: 40 MINUTES
1. Place the washed and picked-over beans in a large saucepan. Cover with 2 inches (or three times their volume) of fresh unsalted water.
2. Bring to a boil, reduce the heat to moderate, and cook for 10 minutes.
3. Drain the beans and cover with 2 inches (or three times their volume) of fresh cool water.
4. Soak for 30 minutes. Discard the soaking water, rinse well, and the beans are ready for cooking.

while to see if the beans are becoming too dry, adding a little boiling water if necessary. When they appear to be done, test as described in the next section.

Mexican cooks never stir the beans while they are cooking.

One problem we have with the Mexican method is that the indigestible sugars that cause flatulence are cooked along with the beans. To circumvent this, drain the cooking broth from the cooked beans and rinse them well in a colander under running water before continuing with a recipe.

COOKING DRIED BEANS

ON TOP OF THE STOVE

The easiest way to cook dried beans is to place the presoaked and drained beans in a large pot, cover them well with tap or bottled water (no salt), bring them to a boil, reduce the heat to a bare simmer, put the cover on slightly ajar, and cook them until tender. A painless way to test for doneness is to press a cooked bean with a fork against a work surface or dish; if it mashes easily, it's done. Or press a slightly cooled cooked bean with your tongue against your front teeth or the roof of your mouth—you want it to be tender but not soft. If there is resistance, cook the beans a little longer and test one again. You can cook the beans with a little vegetable oil, about a tablespoon, to keep them from foaming over.

COOKING DRIED BEANS IN A PRESSURE COOKER

Never cook beans in a pressure cooker unless the pot is no more than half full—and that includes the cooking liquid. Then cook at 15 pounds of pressure for the times indicated in the chart in this chapter. Reduce pressure at the end of the cooking time by running cold water over the cover of the pressure cooker. This will stop the cooking immediately. If you remove the pot from the stove and allow the pressure to reduce gradually, be sure to cut the cooking time shown in the chart by 2 or 3 minutes because the beans continue to cook until the pressure is completely released. Beans have a tendency to foam up in a pressure cooker and clog the valve during cooking. You can prevent this by adding a tablespoon of vegetable oil for each cup of beans before cooking. The oil will also stop loose bean skins from entering the steam escape valve and causing problems.

COOKING DRIED BEANS IN A SLOW COOKER

Slow cookers are perfect for cooking dried beans because beans should be cooked very slowly anyway. Just follow the manufacturer's directions or, better still, put them up in the morning and let them cook unattended at the lowest setting all day. We don't recommend it for those who worry about intestinal gas, but all-day cooking in the slow cooker can waive presoaking. Just add the dried beans to the pot, cover them by 1 inch or more with water, and cook at the lowest setting all day. They will rehydrate and become tender, as in the Mexican no-soak method.

COOKING DRIED BEANS IN A MICROWAVE OVEN—NOT

Don't do it! No matter what the manufacturer's directions say, do not use a microwave to cook dried beans—they need very slow simmering to soften. Use microwave ovens only for reheating cooked bean dishes like soups, stews, and casseroles.

THE FLATULENCE FACTOR AND HOW TO DEAL WITH IT

Beans are notorious for creating gas in the lower intestine. But they are also an invaluable source of dietary fiber. All high-fiber foods contain quantities of com-

---

EQUIVALENT MEASURES FOR COOKING DRIED BEANS

Keep in mind that no matter which method you choose to cook dried beans, they will measure at least twice as much after cooking. The following equivalents are good to keep in mind when planning a meal or cooking in quantity for freezing:

- 1 cup of dried beans will yield 2 to 3 cups of cooked beans (1 to 1¼ pounds)
- 1 cup of dried beans produces four average servings (about ½ cup each)
- 1 pound of dried beans measures 2 cups

APPROXIMATE SOAKING AND COOKING TIMES FOR DRIED BEANS

Note: Use the cooking times given here as a guide. The freshness of the beans will affect timing (the older the beans, the more cooking time they will require). Buy dried beans at a store where turnover is rapid, such as an ethnic market, or ask the proprietor how long he might have had a particular bag of beans on the shelf. Cook, covered, over moderately low heat, at a bare simmer.

TYPE	SOAKING (hours)	COOKING	PRESSURE COOKER (soaked)	(unsoaked)
Adzuki	4	1 hour	15 minutes	20 minutes
Black Beans	4	75 minutes	15 minutes	20 minutes
Black-Eyed Peas	—	30 minutes	—	10 minutes
Lima Beans	4	1 to 1^1/$_2$ hours	20 minutes	25 minutes
Cannellini	4	1 hour	15 minutes	20 minutes
Chickpeas	4	2 to 2^1/$_2$ hours	25 minutes	35 minutes
Dals	—	25 minutes	—	8 minutes
Fava (Broad Beans)	12	3 hours	40 minutes	1 hour
Ful Nabed (Broad)	12	3 hours	40 minutes	1 hour
Great Northern	4	1 hour	15 minutes	20 minutes
Brown Lentils	—	25 minutes	—	10 minutes
Green Lentils	—	30 minutes	—	12 minutes
Red Lentils	—	20 minutes	—	8 minutes
Mung Beans	4	45 minutes to 1 hour		
Split Peas	—	30 minutes	—	10 minutes
Whole Peas	4	40 minutes	15 minutes	20 minutes
Pigeon Peas	—	25 minutes	—	10 minutes
Pink, Calico, Red Mexican Beans	4	1 hour	20 minutes	25 minutes
Pinto Beans	4	1 to 1^1/$_2$ hours	20 minutes	25 minutes
Red Kidney Beans	4	1 hour	20 minutes	25 minutes
White Kidneys	4	1 hour	20 minutes	25 minutes
Small Navy Beans	4	2 hours	25 minutes	30 minutes
Soybeans	12	3 to 3^1/$_2$ hours	30 minutes	35 minutes

Note: Any beans listed in the "Meet the Beans" chapter but not listed here are in the kidney bean family and should be soaked for 4 hours, cooked 1 to 1½ hours, pressure cooked (soaked) for 20 minutes, (unsoaked) for 25 minutes.

plex sugars (indigestible by the human body) called *oligosaccharides,* which are consumed by the bacteria resident in the colon. It is these bacteria, feeding on the oligosaccharides, that create carbon dioxide and other gases. Humans do not have the enzymes in the small intestine required to digest these sugars, but the large intestine's bacteria population devours them.

Through this process beans do produce gas—but no more so than broccoli, cabbage, turnips, cauliflower, onions, garlic, leeks, and many other vegetables and fruits, especially apples, pears, prunes, grapes, unripe bananas, melons, fruit juices, low-calorie jellies and sweets, seeds, and nuts. All should bear the same stigma as beans.

Different people produce different amounts of gas even after eating the same kinds and amounts of foods. A food that does not create much gas in one person can produce large quantities in another—even in the same family. If someone is producing what is perceived as an excessive amount of gas, it could be a result of swallowing a lot of air, eating lots of high-fiber foods, or having an overabundance of ravenous bacteria in the lower intestine.

Happily, gas from beans can be controlled. First, if beans are not a part of your current diet, introduce them gradually. Excessive flatulence is a problem only among those who eat beans rarely—like most Americans. The intestinal tracts of regular, constant consumers of beans adapt quickly—so after only a few days of regularly consuming beans, the gas virtually disappears.

Second, if the water in which you have soaked dried beans is poured off and the oligosaccharides that might still be clinging to them are rinsed off under running water—and if canned beans are drained and rinsed well before they are added to a dish—most of the offending oligosaccharides will be flushed down the kitchen sink, never to be heard from again.

One final note: the dietary fiber in beans can prevent or stave off many diseases of the blood and circulatory system and of the lower intestine, mainly bowel cancer. When you pit the slight embarrassment a little gas might cause in a social situation against the positive health benefits of beans, there's no contest.

MEET THE BEANS

Identifying all the beans available in cans, frozen, or dried can be daunting for the inexperienced bean cook. This chapter describes the most common types plus some of the dried "designer" beans that have recently come on the market. These are not new strains; they have been grown from existing heirloom beans for their appearance, their flavor, and their uniqueness. We note their distinguishing visual qualities, their individual flavors, their culinary uses, a few of their nicknames, some historical background when appropriate, and recommended substitutes.

Most canned and dried beans in the kidney bean family, those whose origins are in Central and South America, have little in taste and texture to distinguish them from their relatives. It's size, color, and tradition that govern the choice of these beans in many recipes. Kidney bean varieties in this extended family—the exotics included—are therefore virtually interchangeable. If the one specified in a recipe isn't on your grocer's shelves, don't despair; pick another of a similar size and general color range. Although the finished dish may not look exactly the same, the taste and texture will not be altered appreciably.

ADZUKI

You may see these beans labeled *azuki, aduki, adsuki, asuki,* or *feijao.* They are very small (¼-inch) oval maroon beans with a thin white racing stripe along the hilum or keel (where the bean is attached to the pod). Grown in Asia for thousands of years, they are eaten fresh, dried, sprouted, and ground into flour in both savory and sweet dishes. Their flavor is somewhat sweet and nutty; the texture is delicate, soft, and nonmealy. Adzuki are 25 percent protein and an excellent source of iron and other minerals, calcium, thiamine, and other vitamins. They are available dried at health food, Asian, and Indian stores. They are available canned under the Eden label at health food stores. One cup dried yields 3 cups cooked. Black beans can be substituted except in dessert recipes.

APPALOOSA

Named for the Appaloosa, a horse that, like the bean, comes from the Palouse, a legume-growing region of the Pacific Northwest. A small, long narrow bean with one end white and the other dark brown with tan striations. Like other kidney and haricot beans, it is rather neutral in flavor and takes to seasonings beautifully, especially those of southwestern and western American cuisine. There are black and white beans also marketed as Appaloosa or New Mexican Appaloosa, but they are different beans known as *Indian grave*. Available only dried. One cup dried yields about 2¹/₂ cups cooked. Appaloosas have the same nutrients as other kidney beans of Central and South American origin.

BLACK BEANS

Also known as *turtle beans, frijoles negros, Mexican blacks,* and *Spanish black beans,* black beans are about ⁵/₈ inch long and kidney shaped. Appearing to be shiny black in color, they are actually very deep purple, as the cooking water will show. This native of South America is used in all Hispanic cuisines, especially for garlicky black bean soup. The distinctive, barely tangy flavor marries well with acidic ingredients, smoked meats, cilantro, onions, and tomatoes. Black beans are a major source of protein in such dishes as Brazilian feijoada and the Caribbean's Moros y Christianos (black beans and rice). Protein content is 23 percent with lots of iron, calcium, and the B vitamins. Black beans are available canned, both unseasoned and seasoned, and as a soup (which can also be used as a sauce, undiluted and heated). One cup dried black beans yields 2 to 2¹/₂ cups cooked.

BLACK-EYED PEAS

Depending on the region, they can be called *brown-eyed peas, black-eyed beans, cowpeas, oea beans, china beans, marble beans,* or *black-eyed suzies.* This is a creamy-colored kidney-shaped bean about ¹/₂ inch long with a purplish black mark surrounding the keel or hilum (thus the name). A native of China, it traveled west via the Silk Route, and Arab traders introduced it to Africa. Slaves brought it to the Western Hemisphere, where it became a staple of plantation diets in the eighteenth century and a favorite in the South. Black-eyed peas have a light, smooth texture and a subtly savory taste. The dried beans' thin skin allows them to be cooked without presoaking (cooking time is 30 minutes). Precooked beans are sold both canned and frozen. They contain 22 percent protein, some iron, calcium, phosphorus, potassium, vitamin B complex, and, unlike most beans, some vitamin A. One cup dried yields a little over 2 cups cooked.

BORLOTTI (SEE CRANBERRY BEANS)

BROAD BEANS (SEE FAVA BEANS)

BROWN BEANS

Although they originated in South America, these are called *Swedish beans* because they are used mostly in Scandinavia, where they find their way into sweetened purees served with game and smoked meats and are used in other earthy dishes. Brown beans (aka *Swedish browns, brune bohne,* and *café au lait beans*) are medium-small, roundish, café-au-lait-colored, and quite sweet. They are available canned on the shelves of some specialty food shops and health food stores. If you can't find them, substitute small white beans or kidney beans. Their nutrient values are the same. One cup dried yields 2 to 2½ cups cooked.

BUTTER BEANS (ALSO SEE LIMA BEANS)

These are really large limas, creamy white beans 1¼ inches long that are coarser in texture and flavor than their smaller, more delicious siblings. They are available canned, and that's a good thing because their strong cooking odor offends many people. Somewhat popular in England, butter beans originated in Central America. Nutrients are pretty much the same as for all South American beans. One cup dried doubles when cooked.

CALYPSO

Sold as *black calypso, orca,* and sometimes *yin-yang* (because this round, medium-size bean is roughly split between black and white). There are a few errant black dots on the white field, which fade to gray when cooked. Not available canned, the dried calypso's earthy flavor is particularly good in hearty, slow-cooked soups like caldo gallego and in stews like the French classic cassoulet. Another bean called *Indian grave* has similar markings but a different shape. Calypsos have the same nutrients as other South American beans. One cup dried yields 2 to 2½ cups cooked.

CANNELLINI (ALSO SEE HARICOT BEANS)

Sometimes called *fasolia* or *white beans.* A member of the haricot family, originally cultivated in Argentina, cannellini are associated mainly with Italian cuisine, especially that of Tuscany. This is a white oval bean, usually ½ inch in length, but smaller varieties (about $^3/_8$ inch) are also canned. The texture is smooth, the flavor somewhat nutty. Nutrient values are the same as for the other beans of South and Central American origin such as kidney. Versatile cannellini can be used in many cooked dishes, especially those from the Mediterranean area, and in purees, salads, and soups. They absorb flavors readily and are a good stand-in for kidney beans of any color. Nutrients are the same as for other kidney beans. One cup dried cannellini yields 2 to $2^1/_2$ cups cooked.

CHANNA DAL

These are $^1/_4$-inch yellow split peas grown and eaten in India and Southeast Asia under the names *chenna, chanai, arhar dal, toor dal, tur, toer, toker, toovar dal, ooloonthoo,* and *pigeon peas.* Because they are hulled, they cook quickly, like lentils. They can be used in purees, in rice, with meat, fried snack foods, and vegetable dishes. Ground, they can substitute for chickpea flour. American yellow split peas offer the same texture, but the flavor is not nearly as nutty. They provide a good source of iron, vitamin B, and protein and are available in Indian and Asian markets. One cup dried yields about $2^1/_2$ cups cooked.

CHICKPEAS

Widely known as *garbanzos* or *ceci,* chickpeas can also be called *hummus beans* and *kabli channa,* depending on the ethnicity of the market. This round, beige-colored bean looks like a ram's head with its horns curled over the ears. The Latin name for the bean, *cicer,* is the basis for the Roman family name of Cicero. About $^3/_8$ inch in diameter, chickpeas are one of the most versatile of all the legumes with their pronounced nutty flavor and firm texture. They originated in North Africa and the Middle East, where they were first cultivated 7,000 or 8,000 years ago, and became a staple of Old World diets. Chickpeas play an important role in the regional cooking of many countries in Europe, Africa, the Middle East, and Asia. They are India's most prominent legume, fried, boiled, roasted, sprouted, made into soups and fritters, ground into flour and made into dumplings, pancakes, and bread, or used to thicken stews and sauces. Perhaps the most popular and familiar dish made from chickpeas is the Middle Eastern puree hummus, flavored with sesame paste (tahini), garlic, oil, and lemon juice. Rich in nutrients, the bean contains large amounts of protein, calcium, iron, and the B vitamins, some of which are in the skins, which we often leave on if they are not loose—and especially when we are pureeing the bean as in hummus. When appearance counts, by all means discard any loose skins. One cup dried chickpeas yields about 3 cups cooked.

CHINA YELLOWS

The other names for these beans also indicate their lovely color: *canarios, sulphur beans* (denotes color, not taste), and *small yellows.* As you've guessed, these are pale yellow—small, plump, and roundish. Their texture, like their color, is buttery smooth; their flavor is equally rich. Alas, their color fades when cooked, but it can be heightened by adding saffron or turmeric to the cooking liquid. Puree with garlic and olive oil and serve alongside something bright in color like roasted red bell peppers. One cup dried yields 2½ cups cooked. China yellows have the same nutrient value as other kidney beans of Central and South American origin.

CHRISTMAS LIMAS

Not a lima bean at all but a very large flat white bean with distinctive purple-brown, batiklike markings that fade unless undercooked. Also known as *Christmas beans, chestnut beans, fagioli della nona (grandma's beans),* or almost any other name a marketer chooses to think up, they have a sweet, chestnutlike flavor that is welcome in stews and ragouts where they soak up a lot of flavor-bearing liquid. Simmered in broth or stock, the drained beans can be tossed with fresh herbs, dried cranberries, and raspberry-flavored vinegar for an unusual salad. Not available canned. One cup dried yields about 2 cups cooked. They are in the kidney bean family with the same nutrient values.

CRANBERRY BEANS

In Italian cookbooks these beans are referred to as *borlotti* or *saluggia.* In other countries they may be known as *Roman, Tuscan, lamon, rosecoco, shell beans, tongues of fire, crab-eye,* or *cargamantos.* They are the reverse of pinto beans in color: a pink skin with beige markings. Although they may be used interchangeably with pinto beans in some recipes, they are a plumper bean with a smoother texture and a slightly more assertive flavor. After cooking, however, they are hard to tell apart; they both turn pink. These delectable beans can be found fresh in pods that bear the same striated markings as pintos in Italian markets and some specialty produce shops. Canned cranberry beans are a rarity on this country's store shelves. Use pintos or cannellini instead. As for nutritive value, they are the same as other kidneys. One cup dried yields 2½ cups cooked.

DAL

Dal or *dhal* is the generic name used in India for all legumes—lentils, peas, or beans.

EUROPEAN SOLDIERS

Also called simply *soldiers* or *red eyes,* these are large white, kidney-shaped beans with a red mark at the hilum or keel depicting a soldier standing at attention. The figure remains even when cooked. Serve them to your army buddies. Nice when drained and tossed, while still hot, with olive oil, Gorgonzola, and fresh sage or rosemary leaves. They make a good substitute for kidney beans, but not vice versa (try cannellini instead). One cup dried yields 2½ cups cooked. Same nutrients as other kidney beans.

FAVA BEANS

Depending on which side of the Atlantic you're on, favas (the Italian name) can be called *faba, broad beans,* or *horse beans.* Elsewhere they are known as *ful medames, ful, ful misri,* or *habas.* Fava was the only bean known to Europe other than the chickpea and lentil before the exploration of the New World and the introduction of the various kidney beans discovered there. Favas are large, ³/₄ inch long, flat, greenish brown to dark brown in color, and sometimes confused with the lima bean by Americans. Favas' skin is tough, so dried beans should be peeled after soaking if the skins haven't loosened and floated to the top. But the texture of dried favas is sandy. We prefer canned beans if fresh aren't available. They come to market in early spring and are delicious eaten raw with a little salt. This is the bean used for the traditional Greek or Middle Eastern street food felafel. In this country it is more likely to be made with chickpeas. Favas' hearty flavor should be matched with equally hearty seasonings and other full-flavored ingredients. Ful nabed is an Egyptian variety of favas that is creamy white in color.

Nutrients in dried or canned favas are the same as in chickpeas. One cup dried favas yields 2 cups cooked.

FLAGEOLET

Aka *chevrier vert,* these are smallish, immature kidney beans that have been removed from their pods when very young. They are very pale green, sometimes almost white. Their light, fresh flavor (like comparing veal to beef) and tender texture make them the caviar of the bean world. They're cultivated mainly in France and Italy, where they are typically paired with lamb, tossed in an herbed vinaigrette, and served cool in an *hors-d'oeuvre varié* or as part of an antipasto plate. They can be found fresh at some gourmet greengrocers and canned, bottled, or dried at specialty food shops. Flageolets are lovely combined with leeks in a gratin. Expensive.

FRENCH NAVY BEANS

Also called *coco blanc,* these small, plump, round white beans have green undertones and jacquard-style visible monochrome veining. They are velvety smooth, buttery textured with a rich bacony flavor that's nothing like the plain old navy beans we all know and work best in purees or baked. Or try cooking them with whole cloves of garlic, then mashing both with a little of the cooking liquid. If unavailable, flageolets could be a stand-in. One cup dried yields 2$\frac{1}{2}$ cups cooked. Nutrient content is the same as other kidney beans.

FRESH GREEN BEANS

What most of us call *string beans* or *snap beans* are really immature kidney beans, the beans barely visible, that we eat pods and all. Green beans were first brought back to Spain from the New World by the conquistadores and their followers not as a food, but as an ornamental flowering plant. The pink and white flowers decorated Spanish gardens for several decades before anyone decided to cook and eat the long green pods. Soon after they became a kitchen staple all over Europe. Green beans are now grown everywhere in the world and come in more than 100 varieties—most no longer with "strings" (the pods first became stringless in 1894). The French covet haricots verts for their delicately flavored, very tender narrow pods. Their price is high at the greengrocer but worth it, every once in a while, as a treat. "French" beans are not the same; they are simply our everyday string beans sliced on an exaggerated diagonal, almost vertically, to make them look as skinny as the French couture originals.

Look for beans of the same size in the market (they'll cook evenly), beans that are crisp, have a slightly fuzzy skin, and snap easily and juicily. Avoid fat, limp, soggy beans or those swollen with seeds. Green beans are 92 percent water, so there are only 30 calories to a cooked cupful. In spite of this they are loaded with potassium, calcium, and phosphorus, plus a heavy dose of vitamin A. Cook beans uncovered to preserve their color.

GARBANZOS (SEE CHICKPEAS)

GREAT NORTHERN BEANS (SEE HARICOT BEANS)

HARICOT BEANS

Haricot beans are the mature dried white seeds of the green bean or string bean (haricot vert in France). They come in a great many varieties, sizes, and colors, with equally varied names like *Great Northern beans, small whites, navy beans, soissons, cannellini,* and *white kidney beans.* The most common are the Great Northern or navy beans, which are ivory white, small ($^3/_8$-inch) ovals, slightly kidney shaped with a thick, tough skin. The most widely used of all the common beans, they are the beans of Boston baked beans, the reason Tuscans are known as *mangia fagioli* or bean eaters, and the bean of choice for French cassoulet. They contain 23 percent protein, 61 percent carbohydrate, as well as iron, calcium, and the B vitamins, among other important nutrients. Cannellini and small whites are the ones you'll usually find in cans. One cup dried yields about $2^1/_2$ cups cooked.

JACOB'S CATTLE BEANS

Called *trout beans* by some, *Anasazi* and *beautiful beans* by others, these large white beans have the advantage of retaining their unique markings, red-purple-maroon blots and circles, even after cooking. They are cooked like other kidney beans, but their fresh flavor, smooth texture, and exciting appearance are more distinctive. Originally the *Anasazi* bean, it was taken from our Southwest to

Spain, then to England, where it became *Jacob's cattle*, then back to America as the *Anasazi* once again. It is a good alternative to cannellini in Italian dishes. One cup dried yields 2¹/₂ cups cooked. Same nutrients as all Central and South American beans.

LABLAB BEANS

This is a nutritious brown bean native to India, now cultivated in Egypt, which only travelers to the Middle East will come across. Rarely exported, they can be grown in a kitchen garden in most parts of the United States.

LENTILS

One of the first food products to be cultivated, the lentil has been grown continuously since fields were first planted by the early inhabitants of southwestern Asia, in the fertile valley of the Indus River. Its diaspora took it first to other lands of the Middle East, then to northeastern Africa, and on to India in one direction and eastern Europe in the other. In the seventeenth century the word for a doubly convex piece of glass was *lens* after the similarly shaped bean. It was lentil porridge that Esau in the Old Testament sold his birthright for (which still sounds good to us: lentils and onions simmered slowly with sesame oil). Lentils are the seeds of a small shrub and are the mainstay of the diets of many underdeveloped countries, providing much of the protein intake. One of the few beans to break the class barrier, lentils can be found in both elegant dishes and peasant fare. Lentils are one of the few dried beans that need no soaking and cook relatively quickly. They contain 25 percent protein and are richly endowed with other nutrients like iron and the B vitamins. There are many varieties of lentil, including the numerous Indian dals, but the main kinds available elsewhere are basically variants of the red, green, and brown. Here's a sampling:

BROWN LENTILS. Slate brown in color, shiny, flat, ¹/₄ inch around, these are the *lentilles blondes* of France and are probably the most flavorful of all lentils. They are simply served with butter in France, olive oil in the Middle East, and rice in other areas, where they can serve as a complete meal. Quick cooking, they should be checked and tested for doneness after 18 minutes. Too long in the pot and they can disintegrate. The supermarket lentils Americans are familiar with are smaller Chinese brown lentils, which have an earthy taste and are not nearly as tasty. One cup dried yields 2 cups cooked.

BROWN MASOOR LENTILS. The lentils found in Indian and Middle Eastern dishes, these are really red lentils in their seed coats. They are too tender to be used in Western dishes. One cup dried yields 2 cups cooked.

FRENCH LENTILS. Aka *Le Puy, du Puy, petite French*. Small, plump, and khaki-colored flecked with dark green and tan markings. Hearty, herby, intensely flavorful. They put all other lentils to shame (they're French, after all!); ideal for salads, stews, and side dishes because the seed coat remains intact when cooked. Lentils labeled "Le Puy" come from a particular tiny area of France; those labeled simply "French" or "du Puy" could signify style and don't necessarily even come from France. One cup dried yields 2 cups cooked.

GREEN LENTILS. Aka *Chilean lentils, lairds, Egyptian lentils*. Dull olive color, small, lens shaped, with a light, fresh, yet luxurious flavor that takes well to a simple herbed vinaigrette, served chilled. Wonderful in soups that are vibrantly seasoned. The cooking time is longer than for other lentils, about 25 to 30 minutes. One cup dried yields 2 cups cooked.

RED LENTILS. Aka *Egyptian lentils, Turkish lentils, split lentils, pink lentils, crimson lentils*. Bright orange-pink, shiny (if oil-polished), tiny, peeled and split horizontally. Used for soups and purees only because they cook so quickly (10 minutes) and disintegrate when you're not watching. Different in flavor from green lentils; much more delicate with a hint of spice.

Whole Red Lentils. Aka *decorticated lentils, petite crimson, masoor dal, ads majroosh, Egyptian lentils*. Salmon colored, 1/4 inch, without seed coat. Cooking time for these is a little longer than for split red lentils, but they can disintegrate just as quickly. To curb disintegration, cook with an acid such as lemon juice or tomato. One cup dried yields 2 cups cooked. When the brown seed coat is left intact, this lentil is called *brown masoor* and can be used in Middle Eastern and Indian recipes that specify brown lentils. Unhulled, it will hold its shape longer. It should not be substituted for brown lentils.

LIMA BEANS

Large, flattish, creamy white to pale green beans that are variously named *butter beans, Madagascar, curry, pole beans, sieva beans,* and *Fordhooks*. There are two distinct species: the 1 1/4-inch-long kind that is native to Central America but reached

Peru thousands of years ago where it was discovered by Spanish explorers who named it after the Peruvian capital and a smaller variety (only $1/2$ inch long) that hails from Mexico and cooks in a much shorter time because of its thinner, more tender skin. After being introduced to Europe in the sixteenth century, the lima traveled to Africa through the slave trade and has become the most important bean on that continent. It became part of the Native American diet early on. Lima beans are available fresh, dried, frozen, and canned. They contain 23 percent protein and are a good source of the B vitamins, iron, calcium, phosphorus, potassium, and the trace minerals. One cup of dried limas yields about 2 cups cooked.

MAINE YELLOW EYES

A small round white bean with a little yellow-brown mark around the keel, which caused it to be dubbed *yellow eye* and *speckle eye*. It has a mild flavor and smooth texture and can be substituted for navy beans or Great Northerns—often with better results. Although there are several beans called *yellow eye*, this one is favored in the state of Maine, where it is considered the finest of the baking beans. One cup dried yields $2^{1}/2$ cups cooked. Nutrients are the same as those for kidney beans.

MOLASSES EYES

A small to medium roundish white bean with a café-au-lait mark at the keel that remains even after cooking. It is this mark that gives it its name and also provides nicknames like *Steuben yellow eye*. Its smooth texture makes it great for baking and for simmering in a sauce. One cup dried yields $2^{1}/2$ cups cooked. Molasses eyes have the same nutrients as all kidney beans.

MUNG BEANS

Call them *moong dal, mung dal, green gram, golden gram,* or *lou teou,* they're still small ($1/4$-inch) round beans with an olive-green seed coat wrapping a yellowish interior. They are sold hulled or unhulled or split. The pods of young mung beans are eaten as a green vegetable. First cultivated in India about 1500 B.C., they soon spread to China. Both countries use their sprouts, which are five times as rich in vitamins A and B as the whole bean and contain the elusive vitamins C and B_{12}. They are the only beans to offer these two critical vitamins. Sprouts may be cooked along with other ingredients or eaten raw in a salad. Mung bean flour is the basis for Chinese bean threads or cellophane noodles. There are also brown and black varieties of the mung bean. Black mungs are called *urad* and are indigenous to Africa, Asia, and the West Indies. The whole bean contains 24 percent protein and 60 percent carbohydrate with barely 2 percent fat and the rest fiber and other nutrients. The sprout contains only 4 percent protein and 7 percent carbohydrate. Fresh sprouts can be found in Asian markets, at produce stands, and in many supermarkets, where they are also sold canned. The dried bean is available at Chinese and Indian markets. One cup dried yields 2 to $2\frac{1}{2}$ cups cooked.

NAVY BEANS (SEE HARICOT BEANS)

PEANUTS

Peanuts are also known as *groundnuts, goobers* (one of the few African words in the English language), *ground peas, goober peas,* and *monkey nuts.*

Per capita, per year, Americans consume 6 pounds of these delectable legumes. That amounts to 4,000,000 pounds a day. More than half of that is in the form of peanut butter, less than a quarter in the form of salted snacks, and another scant quarter as candy.

Peanuts were brought back to Europe from the New World by Spanish explorers in the late fifteenth and early sixteenth centuries. The Portuguese voyagers to South America spread them to Africa. For some 2,000 years before Columbus they were grown for food in South America. A tropical plant not native to North America, they are thought to have come here first via Africa and the slave trade, as black-eyed peas did. But there is evidence that Native Americans in Virginia were already cultivating them when the first colonists arrived in the seventeenth century.

Even before that, 100,000 years ago, they were growing in China, fossilized remains verify. But we don't actually know where they originated.

Today the largest producers are India and China, countries that crush most of the crop for oil and consume the rest of their production themselves; the largest exporter is Nigeria. The United States produces about one-tenth of the world's peanut crop.

Peanut butter came into existence when a St. Louis physician invented it in 1890. It was introduced to the rest of the country at the St. Louis World's Fair in

1904—as a health food. Peanut butter is highly nutritious; it has ample protein (about 8 grams) and carbohydrate (about 6 grams) plus a nice dose of B vitamins, minerals, and fiber per two tablespoons.

Like soybeans, peanuts store oils instead of starch like other beans. Contrary to popular belief, peanuts cause little or no measurable flatulence.

PEAS

The green pea is one of the few vegetables that can withstand freezing and still taste fresh. Thanks to this modern technology, green peas can be eaten all year long. We find the frozen even better than the fresh—unless they come straight from the garden. Canned peas turn grayish in the processing, are mushy, and don't taste like peas at all. Dried peas are another matter—inexpensive, nourishing, and filling, whether the green or yellow variety. Both are wonderful for stick-to-the-ribs soups and smooth purees. Both have a goodly share of iron, protein, calcium, and some vitamins A and B. They were the dried pea of the Middle Ages and of ancient Greece and Rome. The Chinese were the first to eat them fresh. They helped the English peasants survive a famine in 1555, although the peas were the wild kind; cultivated peas appeared in the late sixteenth century. Peas originated in the Middle East and were cultivated there before 6000 B.C., spread throughout the Mediterranean, then on to India and China—but not, surprisingly, to northern Europe.

PIGEON PEAS

Slaves brought these from Africa, which is probably why they are also known as *goongoo beans* or *Congo beans,* but mostly they are called *gandules.* They are the peas used in many of the rice and peas dishes of the Caribbean, especially hoppin' John, offering a creamy texture and slightly nutty flavor. Pigeon peas were first cultivated by the Egyptians some 4,000 years ago. They are sold in cans and sometimes dried in the Hispanic sections of most supermarkets and at health food stores. One cup of dried pigeon peas cooks up to 2 to $2^1/_2$ cups.

PINK BEANS

These are the beans often called for in South American recipes, a pale pinkish beige version of the common red kidney bean. The same red or the pinto bean can be used instead.

PINTO BEANS

A small, oval kidney bean about $^3/_8$ inch long. Originally from South America, it is beige in color with streaks of brownish pink. It gets its name from the Spanish word for "painted," which was also applied to the horse with similar markings. When cooked, it loses its mottled appearance and becomes pink.

RATTLESNAKE BEANS

These are slightly elongated medium-size light brown beans with dark brown veins. The pod is long and twisted with the same markings as the bean. This is a strong, tangy bean good in Mexican and southwestern dishes with assertive seasonings. Because it looks like a pinto, but larger and darker, it is sometimes called a pinto, which it's not. It has much more character—enough to hold its own with the hottest chilies.

RED PEANUT BEANS

A small dark pink bean that looks something like, you guessed it, a roasted red Valencia peanut—and almost tastes like one. Also called *Valencia peanut*. This is an heirloom variety grown in Maine. One of the few beans that can substitute, albeit reluctantly, for French lentils.

ROSECOCO BEANS (SEE CRANBERRY BEANS)

SCARLET RUNNERS

Sometimes called *scarlet emperors,* these are very large, plump, kidney-shaped beans of black-purple with dark purple coloring on one side fading into flecks. They retain their markings when cooked and have a crisp texture that is perfect for salads. Though the beans are a deep, dark purple, they are called scarlet because of the vivid red flowers on the plant. For this reason they are often planted as ornamentals in temperate climates. Use scarlet runners when you want to offset bright colors in a dish, like red or yellow bell peppers, or make a really dramatic presentation. One cup dried yields $2^1/_2$ cups cooked. Same nutrients as other kidney beans.

SMALL REDS

An oxblood-colored bean, small, slightly elongated, and quite bland, so it needs powerful seasonings. Also called *red chili beans* or *Mexican beans.* Good simmered with spicy, smoky sausages and in red beans and rice. One cup dried yields 2½ cups cooked. Nutrients are the same as other kidney beans.

SNOW PEAS

A tender, immature pea that is eaten pod and all. Best eaten raw in salads, blanched briefly, and refreshed in ice water to stop the cooking or quickly stir-fried. The pod is flat and pale green, the texture crisp, and the flavor sweet. Used extensively in Asian dishes, but terrific in many Western salads and soups, and to add flavor and crunch to sandwiches and appetizers. The tender top leaves of the plant, called *pea pod leaves* or *snow pea leaves,* are used in Shanghai, Vietnamese, and other Asian cuisines. They have a delicate flavor when used raw in salads, quickly stir-fried with minced garlic or ginger, or steamed for a minute or two. Available in Asian markets.

SNOWCAP BEANS

Another large white kidney-shaped bean with a tan, red-veined blotch at the keel that persists even when cooked. The name comes from its appearance, that of a snowcapped mountain when held keel down. Snowcaps' flavor is slightly tangy, slightly acidic, with undertones of tomato—which make it a lovely ingredient for salads or pasta sauce. One cup dried yields 2½ cups cooked.

SOYBEANS

Some call them *soya beans.* About the size of a pea and almost as round, they are pale ivory (most common, but also black, green, and brown) and the hardest and most recalcitrant of all the beans, needing the longest soaking and cooking times. The Chinese rightly considered them "miracle beans" and put them to a wide variety of uses. Modern industry has expanded these uses to include soaps, glue, bottle caps, pencils, paint, disinfectants, face powders and creams, linoleum, nitroglycerin, cement, varnish, diesel fuel, plastics, detergents, and fiberboard. Soybeans enter our diets in the form of lecithin emulsifiers, the substance that holds many foods together, extenders, fortifiers, extracts, and proteins. Imitation (analogue) foods are made from them that are almost indistinguishable from the real thing.

This miracle bean probably got its start in Mongolia, where it has been cultivated for more than 5,000 years and is known as "the meat of the soil." Only in the Far East is the soybean an important human food crop; the Chinese and Japanese make so many food products from soybeans that the list is almost endless. Soy milk, Japan's breakfast drink for example, is richer than cow's milk in iron, calcium, and phosphorus—and it's known as "the cow of China." Tofu (soybean curd), tempeh, soy sauce, soy flour, and miso (soybean paste) along with milk are a few of the Asian soy products that have increased in popularity in the West in recent years. Soybeans are eaten fresh, sprouted, in the pod, and dried. The vast U.S. crop is mostly turned into salad oil (the bean is 34 percent oil), margarine, industrial oils, and livestock feed (38 percent of its edible weight is protein). One cup dried soybeans yields 3 cups cooked.

SPANISH TOLOSANA BEANS

Also called *prince beans* and *Dominican red beans.* A large kidney-shaped maroon bean with tan veins used just like kidney beans—but with a smoother texture and brighter flavor. Jacob's cattle or dark red kidney beans can substitute. One cup dried yields 2½ cups cooked. Nutrients are just like other kidney beans.

SUGAR SNAP PEAS

Available in select greengrocers since the early eighties, this crisp and flavorful cross between the English garden pea and the Chinese snow pea is eaten like its Asian parent, pod and all. Unlike the pale green, flat pod of the snow pea, the pod is round, flat, and a deep green, with ripples that hint of the tiny green peas inside. The snap pea is very sweet. Its flavor is best when cooked quickly by steaming, blanching, or stir-frying until just heated through. Overcooked snap peas become limp and taste bland. They should be stringed before being eaten raw or cooked. Still available late in the summer after the last of the garden peas have been picked.

SWEET WHITE RUNNER BEANS

Very large, plump, off-white, kidney-shaped dried beans that are utterly unique with a rich, sweet flavor. The name refers to the way they grow: on a running vine. Look for them under the aliases *white emergo, giant white, gigandes, corona judiones,* and *fabadas.* Best just with olive oil, salt, and pepper, but a little garlic and parsley make a nice addition. The Greeks dip these beans into a garlicky bread and potato dip called *skordalia*. One cup dried yields 2¹/₂ cups cooked. Look for the same nutrient content as all kidney beans.

TEPARI BEANS

Mexican haricot beans used in many regional dishes throughout Mexico. Use haricot beans as a substitute here. See haricot beans for yield and nutrient content.

WINGED BEANS

A distant cousin of the soybean, called the *soybean of the tropics*. Almost every part of this plant is edible, from the mushroom-flavored flowers to the spinach-flavored leaves, the tubers with eight times the protein of cassava or potatoes, and, of course, the pods and beans. Like soybeans, the beans contain an oil that can be processed. They can be made into tofu, milk, and tempeh. The vines can be used for animal fodder. Unlike soybeans, which need a temperate climate, winged beans thrive in the hot, humid tropics—a great protein source for these undernourished areas.

THE
PROTEIN
QUESTION

All living tissue, both plant and animal, contains protein. Proteins are essential for the formation, maintenance, repair, rehabilitation, and growth of human muscle, connective tissue, blood plasma and hemoglobin, the skin, its keratin, nails, hair, the enzymes, hormones, and antibodies that regulate many of the body's most important functions.

The substances in every cell in our bodies, the very same cells that carry our genetic codes (DNA and RNA) and tell them how to replicate themselves, all require protein enzymes for their structure and composition.

All the animal proteins are relatively high in fat and calories. Even some vegetables contain measurable fat: soybeans, nuts, seeds, and corn, for instance. But it is negligible in comparison to the animal sources.

Nutritionists tell us, correctly, that only animal protein is complete, that it is the only food source that contains all the essential amino acids, 9 of the more than 22 in human tissue.

Nutritionists further claim that the proteins in beans are not as good or good for us as the proteins in animal sources. Even some vegetarians believe this claim of protein inferiority and continue to spread the myth. But it's not true.

The proteins in our diet are needed to help supply and maintain the variety of proteins in our bodies. Proteins are made up of amino acids, chains of carbon, hydrogen, oxygen, and nitrogen. These amino acids, resident in our bodies, combine in endless ways to form the proteins that are the complex building blocks of life.

The protein we eat cannot be stored by our bodies, so a new stock must be acquired daily. But where should this stock come from, animal sources or vegetable?

It doesn't matter in the least.

Most of the 22 amino acids needed for protein synthesis can be manufactured inside our bodies. Eight must come from outside. All eight of these so-called essential amino acids must be present to synthesize protein. If just one of the eight is missing, the manufacturing process stops cold.

Each food has its own unique amino acid pattern that consists of a little more of one and a little less of another. Animal or vegetable, *they all contain the essential amino acids our bodies need,* but in varying quantities. Though the pattern may be different, each and every one of the amino acids is present and accounted for.

So animal protein is not superior to vegetable protein for keeping the body in nitrogen balance.

Nitrogen is one of the leading materials from which the body builds protein. If you take in more nitrogen than you lose through sweat, urine, and feces, or an equal amount, you are said to be in nitrogen balance and receiving enough protein from your diet.

Numerous studies have proved that protein, even when derived from a single source (such as beans, potatoes, cereal, rice, or corn), keeps the body in nitrogen balance as well as milk does (milk has the most appropriate amino acid pattern for humans). Even though the amino acid pattern in these plant foods is completely different from that of milk, the body doesn't care. It goes on manufacturing the proteins it needs anyway.

It makes perfect sense that early humans could not eat a balanced diet. Some days they could find all the vegetables they needed to survive. The next day nothing. Then they would eat meat or birds. If they lived near water, maybe some shellfish or fish. In other words, they ate only what they could get their hands on—whatever they could gather, hunt, or grab. If Stone Age man's body had not been designed to adjust to the seeming whims and caprices of the food supply, not one of us would be here today.

Our way of life may have changed considerably over the past hundred thousand years, but our body chemistry, our genetics, has remained the same. The world we live in today and the world for which we were designed are completely discordant. Our bodies are incredibly efficient machines made to survive under the most inhospitable, hostile circumstances—yet they can be turned into worthless junk if managed improperly.

Therefore, protein complementarity (carefully balancing our protein sources) is a completely unnecessary practice even though most of the great ancient civilizations unconsciously practiced it. They consumed 80 percent grain with 20 percent legumes (allowing a balanced amino acid pattern). A diet of 60 percent grain, 35 percent legumes, and 5 percent dark green leafy vegetables would be even better. Yet even this proportion is unnecessary when beans are part of the diet.

Forget protein complementarity. You can get all the amino acids you need to manufacture proteins in your body even if you eat nothing but beans.

Of course, we're not recommending you do that. Beans don't have two important vitamins, C and D, and very little A; C and A are offered by many other vegetables and fruits; D is synthesized by the body from sunlight. What we *are* suggesting is that you add a lot more beans to your diet. Beans are very good for you. They'll help control your weight, combat obesity and diabetes, help stave off degenerative diseases (those not caused by bacteria and viruses) or slow their progression, and lessen the risk of sudden death due to heart attack. A 1 percent decrease in serum cholesterol results in a 2 percent decrease in the risk of coronary heart disease—see page 40 to understand how the dietary addition of only $^1/_2$ cup of cooked beans daily can reduce your total cholesterol an average of 11.7 percent. Beans also help resist colon and other cancers, keep the veins and arteries free-flowing, and provide you with an adequate supply of fiber along with an abundance of other nutrients necessary to keep the body chemistry functioning smoothly.

What great dividends from this mighty little inexpensive legume! And now that you're about to learn how to incorporate them into your everyday meals with a minimum of fuss, you're ready to enter the wonderful delicious world of beans.

WHAT'S
SO GOOD
ABOUT
BEANS?

Except for snap beans (green beans, snow peas, and sugar snap peas, which are low in protein but high in vitamins A and C), beans—shell beans, the kind that are dried—whether dried, canned, frozen, or fresh out of the pod, are almost solid protein, carbohydrate, and fiber. Other vegetables are mostly fluid.

1 serving of beans (¹/₂ cup)—3¹/₂ to 4 ounces, or 100 grams:

- contains 111 to 118 calories
- contains 20 percent to 25 percent crude protein
- contains rich quantities of the B vitamins
- is comparable to liver and raw wheat germ in folic acid content
- can have as much thiamine as beef liver, especially lima beans
- exceeds peanut butter (another legume) in protein content
- supplies as much as 40 percent of the minimum daily requirement for thiamine and pyridoxine and significant amounts of niacin as well
- contains a rich source of iron, 50 percent of the minimum daily requirement for men and 25 percent of the minimum daily requirement for women
- is an important source of calcium and phosphorus
- contains abundant potassium, which regulates fluid balances in the body

And beans have positive effects on many common ailments: allergies, cancer, cardiovascular problems, diabetes, constipation, hemorrhoids, gallstones, high blood pressure, and high cholesterol.

But the big health news is that beans can play a major role in lowering cholesterol. After a study widely reported in the nation's press in the summer of 1995 claimed that *soybean protein* could significantly lower LDL (bad) cholesterol, health-conscious consumers rushed to sweep soybean products off the shelves.

What the initial articles did *not* report was that you'd have to ingest about *3 pounds of tofu*—which contains a lot of fat—*a day* to have the effect claimed in the research study. Easier said than done. Especially when only about ¹/₂ *cup* of canned beans (infinitely more palatable than tofu, soy milk, textured soy protein, or soy flour, and containing almost no fat) will lower LDL counts equally or *better* without the consequent weight gain—which can be just as dangerous to your health as high cholesterol.

As recounted in the *New England Journal of Medicine,* subjects in the analyzed reports (the analysis was done by the University of Kentucky and paid for in part by Nutrition Technologies of St. Louis, which makes a highly concentrated form of soy protein) were given 47 grams of soy protein a day in order to reduce cholesterol an average of 9.3 percent. But another, earlier study (done by another University of Kentucky team of scientists) in the *Journal of the American College of Nutrition* found that "canned beans in amounts varying from 69 to 150g decreased total cholesterol in the range of –1.4 percent to –16.3 percent, with a median of *– 11.7 percent*" [our italics].

That's less than a 10 percent reduction from soy protein against almost 12 percent for canned beans. We like tofu—but not enough to eat 3 pounds a day. We don't particularly like the taste of soy milk—especially if we have to drink more than 12 8-ounce glasses a day! Tempeh—the most palatable of soy products—is so low in soy protein that you would need the stomach capacity of an elephant to consume enough to make a significant dent in your cholesterol.

Contrast these figures: One can (15 ounces) of beans weighs in at 425 grams— that's a scant 2 cups. The research in the JACN *study finds that 69 to 150 grams a day does the trick. That translates into only ¹/₃ to ²/₃ of a cup of canned beans. Easy enough to eat, delicious and quick to prepare—especially if made according to any of our recipes!*

In an article in *The New York Times* following the soy protein announcement, food reporter Suzanne Hamlin said, "Given the health statistics, food technologists are now scrambling to incorporate *synthetic soy protein* [our italics] into manufactured food. All soy products are made from crushed soybeans, which by themselves taste bland and are time-consuming to cook."

We wonder why these same food technologists "scrambling" to come up with manufactured foods incorporating synthetic soy protein (we have read nowhere in any scientific report that synthetic soy protein is as good as natural) aren't putting the same effort into promoting canned beans. We also wonder why the media never reported the earlier canned bean study.

Canned beans already exist. They're inexpensive, convenient, and have been proven to control and lower cholesterol even better than soy protein. Drained and rinsed thoroughly, they present minimal flatulence problems. They are *not* insipid-tasting like soy products and take only 2 minutes to heat and eat. They don't even require cooking for a salad, cold soup, or a spread or dip. They contain almost no fat, are filled with bountiful quantities of valuable protein, fiber, vitamins, minerals, and other nutrients to keep your whole body healthy—in addition to your cardiovascular system.

What more could you ask from a humble, delicious food?

INGREDIENTS AND TECHNIQUES

INGREDIENTS

Start with the best ingredients you can afford, the freshest you can find, the real things like Parmigiano-Reggiano (only Parmesan cheese from the region around Parma in northern Italy can use this appellation) and a good brand of olive oil. It's the quality of ingredients that makes the difference with simple food.

OLIVE OIL. When it comes to olive oil, we do not specify which kind to use in our recipes. The kind you like best is the kind to use. If that means extra-virgin, use it. If, like us, you like a milder olive flavor, use pure olive oil. Olive oil is never the main ingredient, so it needs to be simply harmonious with the rest of the components of a recipe.

Use Spanish, French, Italian, Greek, or some of the newer California extra-virgin oils; use even the hard-to-find lighter virgins from Morocco, Turkey, Tunisia, Lebanon, or Israel. Just be sure they are the best you can find for the money.

The supermarket brands of refined olive oil like the old standbys Berio and Bertolli and the more recent arrival Colavita are the ones we reach for most often, especially for all-purpose cooking (the smoking point is higher than that of unrefined extra-virgin oils). These commercial brands also package extra-virgin and light olive oils. If you are being economical, by all means choose the commercial Italian brands from the supermarket shelf and you won't go wrong.

OTHER OILS. As an alternative to olive oil, we often choose canola oil or one of the flavored olive or vegetable oils when appropriate. But olive oil is always our first choice, especially for salads, because of its distinctive flavor and health qualities.

TOMATOES. Canned whole Italian tomatoes are a wonderful stand-in for fresh tomatoes in a cooked dish; when vine-ripened tomatoes are not in season, the canned variety can offer a similar intense flavor; besides, they are already peeled, saving lots of preparation time.

SEASONINGS. Maggi seasoning, a dark brown liquid seasoning which you'll find in any supermarket in little long-necked bottles, is indispensable as far as we are concerned. Salad dressing, especially vinaigrette, without it seems uninteresting. A few dashes can lend a nutty distinction to almost any recipe. Maggi is as ubiquitous on the Swiss dining table as salt and pepper. We use the 27-ounce size we find in Asian markets; it's only 2½ times the price of the 2-ounce supermarket bottles.

Sprinkle on more or less salt according to taste or diet. This goes for canned chicken broth as well: use low-sodium brands if you prefer or make your own. It's up to you.

Fresh herbs are available almost year-round in the produce bins of supermarkets and specialty greengrocers. Use them if you can get them. Substitute half the amount of dried herbs for the fresh *only* when the herb is a seasoning. If it's an essential ingredient, as fresh basil is in pesto, don't use the dried kind. Seeds, such as fennel, dill, coriander, and others, should never be used as an alternative to the fresh herb; the flavor is often completely different and can ruin a recipe.

Dried commercially packaged spices should be replaced every few months because they lose strength standing on the market or pantry shelf. If you have access to a store that offers whole spices, grind them as you need them and you'll be sure of their potency. An inexpensive electric coffee grinder is a good investment for this purpose.

OLIVES. Canned American black olives don't appear in our recipes because they're tasteless. Canned or bottled green olives, stuffed or not, are fine, but loose, plump Mediterranean ones available at many specialty food stores and deli counters are less salty and have more flavor. Any Mediterranean country's salted, dried, or oil-cured black olives are splendid. Each has its own personality, so try to use only those specified in a particular recipe.

CUCUMBERS. We prefer Kirbys, the pickling cukes. They're not waxed, need not be peeled, and are wonderfully crisp. Of course you can use the long, European seedless variety, but we like the flavor of the Kirbys, and besides, they're less expensive.

BEANS. As for canned beans, we could recommend specific brands, but no producer seems to have nationwide distribution. Progresso and Goya are the brands found most easily on the East Coast, parts of the Midwest, the South, and California. Other brands have spotty distribution, and you'll have to seek out your favorite. Try ethnic markets or the Hispanic section of your supermarket for the widest choice of beans, brands, and can sizes. Health food stores may carry some varieties of canned beans you might not find in your local market.

Canned beans customarily come in 10-ounce, 15-ounce, and 19-ounce cans. We say *customarily* because these measurements can vary by an ounce or two, depending on the canner. If a recipe calls for a 19-ounce can of chickpeas, for instance, and you can find only 20-ounce cans, the extra ounce will not throw off the final product. Put it all in; don't bother to measure and weigh. The standard 15-ounce can we might specify can be upped to 16 ounces by some canners. Don't worry; use the whole can. A 15-ounce can is approximately 2 cups of cooked beans; a 19-ounce can yields almost 2½ cups; the 10-ounce can is over 1 cup.

In this cookbook we call for only canned, frozen, or fresh beans. But as we've already suggested, you certainly can soak and cook dried beans and then measure out the specified amount—if canned varieties are not available or if you'd like to try one of the "designer" beans for a more interesting color, texture, or taste in a dish. For convenience, we suggest you cook dried beans in large quantities and freeze them in 2-cup containers for future use. Unused portions may be refrozen. Home-cooked and frozen beans can last a year or more.

TECHNIQUES

All the recipes you'll find in this book can be served in 30 minutes or less—often a lot less. But a great deal depends on how adept you are with a paring knife, a chef's knife, a sieve, a masher, a food mill, a processor, or a blender. The cooking times in our recipes are precise; the time it takes to assemble and prepare raw ingredients, (chopping, mincing, slicing, paring, pureeing, etc.) will vary according to your skills. Estimated times for these chores are taken into account based on how long it takes *us* to accomplish them. These recipes are fast, however, even if you lack the skills and dexterity of a professional cook.

PUREEING CANNED BEANS

Many recipes in this book call for pureed beans. This is easily accomplished with canned beans (or home-cooked dried beans) and usually requires no additional liquid. Simply drain and rinse canned beans (best done in a sieve or colander) and whirl in a food processor or blender, stopping several times to scrape down the sides, until the beans become a smooth paste. This should take only 1 or 2 minutes, depending on the amount of beans you are pureeing. Use this method when pureeing beans with other ingredients, dry or liquid. You may also puree frozen beans in a blender or processor without thawing by breaking the frozen block into small chunks and pureeing in their frozen state.

Pureeing beans in a food mill or pressing them through a sieve will produce slightly less volume because the skins might not go through the perforations. The lesser quantities are not significant enough to change the result of a recipe.

Volume of puree from drained and rinsed beans:
<u>From canned beans:</u>
1 15-ounce* can yields about 1$\frac{1}{2}$ cups puree
1 19-ounce* can yields a scant 2 cups puree

<u>From home-cooked beans:</u>
2 cups rinsed and drained beans yield about 1$\frac{1}{2}$ cups puree

---

* Some canners put up beans in 16- or 20-ounce cans. The contents will yield slightly more puree than the smaller cans, but the increase is not enough to make a difference in a recipe.

APPETITE
TEASERS

Bean and Anchovy Puffs

MAKES 24 TO 30

We use anchovies a lot, mostly as a seasoning. They find their way into stews (both meat and fish), sauces, cocktail spreads, and sandwiches—just as the Southeast Asians use fish sauce. These puffs, which should be served hot with drinks, use anchovy paste to add a sharp, salty flavor to the bean paste they're combined with. Use less anchovy paste the first time if you're not sure your guests will like it. The beans, of course, add substance and a nutty flavor of their own. Which brings us to the choice of beans. We don't specify. You can use chickpeas, cannellini, black, pink, red, brown, pinto, or black-eyed peas. Even color makes no difference because the filling is enclosed in puff paste. So you can use any puree you happen to have around, as long as it's unseasoned or the original seasonings are compatible with the anchovies.

Preheat the oven to 375°.

In a small bowl, stir together the anchovy paste, bean puree, mayonnaise, garlic, and pepper until well combined.

On a lightly floured surface, roll out each sheet of pastry into a 14-inch square. Trim off excess to make them even.

Brush off excess flour and spread the anchovy mixture evenly over one pastry sheet right to the edges. Cover with the remaining pastry sheet and gently press the sheets together.

With a pastry wheel or sharp knife, cut the pastry into bite-size pieces, about 1 inch square, and with the tines of a fork press the edges of the pastries together, leaving score marks.

Arrange the squares on lightly greased baking sheets and brush the tops with the egg wash. Bake the pastries until puffed and golden, about 12 to 15 minutes. Serve hot on a napkin-lined platter.

3 tablespoons anchovy paste

3 tablespoons unseasoned bean puree

3 tablespoons best-quality bottled mayonnaise

1 large garlic clove, minced

1/2 teaspoon freshly ground pepper

1 1-pound package frozen puff pastry sheets, thawed

1 large egg, beaten with 1 tablespoon water for an egg wash

Bean, Shrimp, and Cream Cheese Puff Paste Roulade

SERVES 10 AS AN HORS D'OEUVRE, 6 AS A FIRST COURSE, OR 4 AS A
LUNCH OR SUPPER MAIN COURSE

We love foods that are wrapped, folded, stuffed, rolled, or filled—foods that are hidden inside other foods. We have made them for every course of a meal (not the same meal!) from first to last. This one is a preamble course, a pastry roll combining a crisp outer texture with a soft, velvety filling devised to serve with drinks or as an appetizer because of its bright, piquant flavor. But nothing says it couldn't stand as a luncheon or light supper dish cut into four portions if that appeals. Just add a salad.

1 8-ounce package cream
   cheese, softened

1/2 pound small shrimp,
   cooked, peeled, and
   chopped

2 teaspoons drained bottled
   horseradish or to taste

1/4 teaspoon cayenne pepper
   or to taste

1 15-ounce can small white
   beans, drained and rinsed

salt and freshly ground pepper to taste

1 sheet (about 1/2 pound)
   frozen puff pastry, thawed

milk for brushing pastry

1/4 cup freshly grated
   Parmesan cheese

Preheat the oven to 400°.

In a bowl, stir together the cream cheese, shrimp, horseradish, and cayenne. Fold in the beans and season with salt and pepper.

On a lightly floured surface, roll the puff pastry into a 16- by 12-inch rectangle. Spread the filling to within 1 inch of all 4 sides. Brush the exposed edges with milk and fold the short sides in over the filling. Now roll up the pastry, starting with one long side, making sure the ends are tucked in as you roll.

Transfer the roulade to a buttered baking sheet, seam side down. Brush the top of the roulade with more milk and sprinkle it with the Parmesan. Bake the roulade in the middle of the oven for 25 minutes or until it is puffed and golden. Let it cool and with a very sharp knife slice it into 10 rounds for hors d'oeuvres, 6 rounds for a first course, or 4 pieces as a luncheon or supper dish.

Garlicky Pureed Chickpea Dip with Cucumber and Yogurt

MAKES ABOUT 2 CUPS

Combining garlic, yogurt, and cucumbers as a soothing, cooling dressing for a pita sandwich is a Greek and Middle Eastern culinary tradition. We like it thickened with bean puree so that it clings to raw vegetables, bread sticks, crackers, and toasted pita triangles on a buffet table. We add chilies to liven things up a bit and cilantro leaves for a clean, fresh fragrance. We've also used this dip as a dressing for a chopped salad or as a sauce for grilled chicken or fish, thinned with a little more yogurt. In other words, make it, taste it, and let your imagination take over from there.

In a food processor, puree the garlic, chickpeas, jalapeño, cilantro, cumin, and salt, stopping to scrape down the sides, until smooth.

In a bowl, stir together the cucumber and yogurt, add the chickpea puree, and combine the mixture well.

The dip can be made 1 day in advance and kept covered and chilled.

2 large garlic cloves, chopped

1 cup rinsed and drained canned chickpeas

1 fresh jalapeño or serrano chili, seeded, deveined (wear rubber gloves), and chopped

$^1/_2$ cup firmly packed cilantro leaves

$^1/_2$ teaspoon ground cumin

$^1/_2$ teaspoon salt or to taste

1 large cucumber (preferably Kirby), finely chopped (about 1$^1/_2$ cups)

1 cup plain yogurt

Southwestern Kidney Bean, Chili, and Cheese Dip with Beer

MAKES ABOUT 4¹/₂ TO 5 CUPS

One way to use leftover beer is in this zesty cheese dip. Don't use dark beer, but a light-colored variety with just enough tangy flavor. It can be fresh or flat—it's not the bubbles that add the flavor. We use a combination of cheddar and Monterey Jack in this recipe, but any semihard cheese such as Swiss or Edam could be substituted.

2 cups grated sharp cheddar cheese (about ¹/₄ pound)

2 cups grated Monterey Jack cheese (about ¹/₄ pound)

1 10-ounce can kidney beans, drained, rinsed, and pureed

1 tablespoon vegetable or olive oil

1 medium onion, minced

¹/₂ teaspoon ground cumin

¹/₂ teaspoon dried oregano, crumbled

salt and freshly ground pepper to taste

³/₄ cup beer

¹/₂ cup drained canned tomatoes, finely chopped

1 pickled jalapeño chili, minced (wear rubber gloves)

In a bowl, mix together the cheeses and pureed beans and set aside.

In a large saucepan or skillet over moderate heat, bring the oil to rippling and in it cook the onion, stirring, until it is softened and beginning to color, about 5 minutes. Add the remaining ingredients, reduce the heat to moderately low, and simmer the mixture, uncovered, for 5 minutes. Add the reserved cheese/bean mixture ¹/₂ cup at a time, stirring after each addition until the cheeses are melted and incorporated.

Serve warm with tortilla chips.

Red Bean Fritters with Monterey Jack and Cilantro

MAKES ABOUT 18. SERVING 4 TO 6

We've cooked up one of our favorite Mexican flavor combinations in a new guise: savory, spicy, melt-in-your-mouth fritters. They're easy to make, and they look pretty on the plate surrounding a dollop of sour cream in which is nestled your favorite red or green salsa. A good idea for brunch, lunch, a light supper, or first course.

In a large mixing bowl, whisk together the cornmeal, flour, baking powder, cayenne, salt, and cumin until well combined. Whisk in $1/2$ cup cilantro, milk, and egg yolk. Stir in the cheese and beans.

In another bowl, beat the egg whites until they hold soft peaks and fold them gently but thoroughly into the bean mixture.

In a large skillet or sauté pan over moderately high heat, bring $1/8$ inch of oil to rippling and, working in batches, drop heaped tablespoons of the batter into the hot oil, flattening them slightly.

Fry the fritters for 1 minute on each side or until they are golden brown, and drain them on paper towels. Keep the fritters warm in a 225° oven until all are fried and drained.

Garnish each serving of 3 or 4 fritters with a dollop of sour cream, a spoonful of red or green salsa, and some of the remaining cilantro. Serve additional sour cream and salsa at the table.

$1/2$ cup yellow cornmeal

$1/4$ cup all-purpose flour

$1/4$ teaspoon baking powder

$1/4$ teaspoon cayenne pepper

$1/4$ teaspoon salt or to taste

$1/2$ teaspoon ground cumin

$1/2$ cup minced cilantro leaves plus 2 tablespoons for garnish

$1/3$ cup milk

1 large egg yolk

1 cup (about $1/4$ pound) Monterey Jack cheese (plain or with hot chilies) in $1/4$-inch dice

1 cup drained, rinsed canned red beans, patted dry with paper towels

2 large egg whites

canola or vegetable oil for frying

sour cream and red or green salsa for serving if desired

White Bean Dip with Coarse Mustard, Horseradish, and Dill

MAKES ABOUT 2 CUPS

People are always on the lookout for new dips to serve with the ever-popular crudités at cocktail parties. This bean-based dip has fewer calories than most made with a mayonnaise or cheese foundation and yet is just as savory and satisfying. Try it. We think it will become a party staple for you as it is for us.

1 15-ounce can white beans, drained and rinsed

½ cup low-fat or nonfat plain yogurt

¼ cup coarse-grained mustard or ¼ cup Dijon mustard combined with 1 teaspoon black mustard seeds, lightly crushed

¼ cup snipped fresh dill

2 tablespoons bottled horseradish

2 tablespoons chopped onion

salt and freshly ground pepper to taste

In a food processor, blend everything together, pulsing several times and scraping down the sides, until the mixture is smooth.

Transfer to a serving bowl and serve with a selection of raw vegetables.

Note: We like this dip thick and clingy (to save our guests from drips), but if you would like a creamier consistency, just add more yogurt, a tablespoonful at a time, until the texture is to your liking.

Chilled White Beans with Chinese Peanut Sauce

SERVES 6 AS A FIRST COURSE

We use pureed beans in this sauce and then serve it on whole beans—a double dose of beans that is spicy, pungent, and satisfying. We've brightened it with ginger, loads of cilantro, and chili oil. You can serve it on noodles (omitting the whole beans) as they do in Chinese restaurants. To turn it into a main dish, julienned strips of cold poached or grilled boned chicken breast or boiled and chilled shrimp can be added. Note: The sauce alone can be used to add sparkle and savor to many grilled dishes—especially grilled fish.

In a food processor, combine 1 cup of the beans with the garlic, ginger, cilantro, oils, peanut butter, soy sauce, sugar, and rice vinegar. Pulse several times, scraping down the sides, and puree until smooth (add a little hot water if a thinner sauce is desired). The sauce keeps for 1 month in a tightly covered container in the refrigerator.

In a serving bowl, toss the remaining beans with the sauce, the scallions, and the cucumber. Sprinkle with the toasted sesame seeds and serve.

2 19-ounce cans white kidney beans or cannellini, drained, rinsed, and chilled

6 large garlic cloves, coarsely chopped

2 tablespoons chopped peeled fresh ginger

2 cups chopped fresh cilantro leaves (about 1 large bunch)

1 tablespoon peanut oil

1 tablespoon Asian toasted sesame oil

1 tablespoon hot chili oil or sesame oil mixed with $1/4$ teaspoon cayenne pepper

$1/2$ cup smooth unsweetened peanut butter

$1/2$ cup light soy sauce

2 tablespoons sugar

3 tablespoons rice vinegar or to taste

3 scallions, both white and green parts, thinly sliced on a diagonal

1 Kirby cucumber, unpeeled, cut into julienne strips

2 tablespoons toasted sesame seeds for garnish if desired

Puree of White Beans with Roasted Garlic and Rosemary

Of the many ways to eat garlic, roasted is one of our favorites. Just squeeze it from its skin and spread it on bread or use it to flavor a multitude of dishes like mashed potatoes or this bean puree. We use a whole head, but if you're not garlic freaks like we are, cut it down to a spartan 5 or 6 cloves—keeping in mind that the longer garlic cooks, the less powerful it is. Roasted, it has a mild, nutty flavor.

1 15-ounce can white beans or cannellini, drained and rinsed

2 tablespoons chicken broth or water

1 teaspoon coarse salt or to taste

2 tablespoons fresh rosemary leaves

1 head of oven-roasted garlic (recipe follows), the cloves squeezed from their skins

2 tablespoons olive oil

$1/2$ teaspoon freshly ground pepper or more to taste

Put all the ingredients into a food processor and blend, pulsing several times and scraping down the sides, until smooth. Add more olive oil or broth if you like a creamier consistency.

Serve with toasted pita triangles as a first course, as a dip with raw vegetables, or as a spread on $1/8$-inch-thick slices of daikon radish or slightly thicker slices of cucumber.

Oven-Roasted Garlic

1 head of garlic

1 teaspoon olive oil

salt and freshly ground pepper to taste

Preheat the oven to 325°.

Slice off the top quarter of the head of garlic, drizzle with the olive oil, and sprinkle with salt and pepper. Wrap in foil and bake until the cloves are soft and creamy, about 40 to 50 minutes. Cool in the foil or unwrap.

When cool, break the head apart and squeeze each clove from its skin. Roasted garlic can be made up to 3 days in advance and kept chilled in a tightly closed container.

Steamed and Salted Winged Beans

SERVES 6 AS A FIRST COURSE OR A CROWD AS FINGER FOOD WITH DRINKS

Our daughter, Abby, took us to a vegetarian Japanese restaurant in Los Angeles where fresh soybeans are served in their pods. The beans are simply steamed and salted and brought to the table at room temperature. We ate them like artichoke leaves, squeezing the beans from their stringy, tough pods with our teeth. They were delicious. We've made them since, at home. Just as good. When we discovered winged beans at an Asian food market, we decided to cook and serve them the same way. Even better. Winged beans have the same nutty flavor and tooth-resistant tenderness as soybeans, but their pods are completely edible, so you're consuming a lot of extra nutrients left behind with soybean pods—not to mention an indescribably mysterious flavor.

On a steamer rack, steam the beans over boiling water, covered, until the beans are tender but still crisp, about 10 minutes. Transfer the beans to a serving bowl and sprinkle with salt. Toss well and serve warm.

1^1/$_2$ **pounds winged beans, trimmed and cut into 2-inch lengths**

salt to taste

BREAD
SPREADS

These are spreadable seasoned purees of beans and other ingredients with minimal fat. They have a lower calorie, high fiber, higher nutrient content than either butter or olive oil. The flavors range in depth from mildly mysterious to tangy to fiery and powerful. And they're even good for you.

Wonderfully versatile, bread spreads can stand in for an appetizer, be served with drinks, be turned into pasta sauces, give a pleasant jolt to soups and stews, add extra zest to vegetables and potatoes, and do things we haven't even thought of yet. See the list of ideas at the end of this chapter. Yes, something good happens whenever bread spreads meet up with food.

But best of all, they're a surefire alternative for butter to spread on crackers, rolls, or slices of a great rustic loaf of bread.

Black Bean Tapenade with Tuna

MAKES A LITTLE MORE THAN 2 CUPS

The classic tapenade is a puree made by blending oil-cured black olives, anchovies, garlic, and capers. We've added black beans and a few other ingredients that are not traditional—but then again neither is the taste or the texture. We think our tapenade is an improvement. It certainly is delicious spread on toasted French bread, but more delicious still spread on poached fresh cod or used as a dressing for sliced tomato and onion salad, even as a sauce for pasta or mixed with $1/2$ cup mayonnaise as a dip for crudités. It has the intense flavors of Provence combined with American ingenuity.

1 cup firmly packed drained Niçoise or other oil-cured black olives

1 cup canned black beans, drained and rinsed

6 canned flat anchovy fillets or more to taste

1 6.5-ounce can solid white tuna, drained and flaked

3 tablespoons drained bottled capers

3 tablespoons chopped fresh parsley or basil leaves

$1/2$ teaspoon freshly ground pepper or more to taste

juice of $1/2$ lemon

2 large garlic cloves, chopped

3 tablespoons basil-flavored oil or olive oil

On a cutting board, crush the olives lightly with a metal meat pounder or the flat side of a large knife and discard the pits.

In a food processor, puree the olives with the black beans. Add the remaining ingredients and puree the mixture well, stopping once or twice to scrape down the sides.

Transfer to an earthenware crock or small bowl and serve the tapenade as a spread for toasted French bread slices (croustades).

Note: In the unlikely event you have leftover tapenade, spread a thin film of olive oil over the top, cover tightly with plastic wrap, and refrigerate for up to 1 week.

Black-Eyed Pea, Tomato, and Mustard Green Spread

MAKES ABOUT 3 CUPS

Mustard greens—sautéed or stewed—are often served in the American South as a vegetable side dish. We like to use them raw in salads, their pungent bite adding another dimension to the usual greens. In this recipe the raw leaves, shorn of their stems and ribs, are combined with another southern staple, black-eyed peas, for a spread that's deliciously spicy and not at all reminiscent of southern cooking.

In a food processor, blend all the ingredients, pulsing several times and scraping down the sides, until the mixture is smooth.

Transfer to a bowl and serve with triangles of cocktail rye, thin slices of toasted French bread, or crackers. Or serve as a dip with potato chips, tortilla chips, or raw vegetables.

The spread can be packed into a container with a tight-fitting lid and chilled until ready to serve. It will keep covered and chilled for up to 1 week.

$1/4$ cup chopped shallot

1 teaspoon Dijon mustard

1 teaspoon freshly grated lemon zest

1 15-ounce can black-eyed peas, drained and rinsed

$1/2$ pound mustard greens, tough stems and center ribs discarded, the leaves coarsely shredded

2 large plum tomatoes, peeled, seeded, and coarsely chopped

1 tablespoon olive oil

1 scallion, both white and green parts, chopped

$1/2$ teaspoon salt or to taste

$1/2$ teaspoon freshly ground pepper

Garlicky Chickpea and Cilantro Pesto

MAKES ABOUT 1³/4 CUPS

This is one of our favorite spreads—our refrigerator never seems to be without a freshly made jar of it. Sometimes we combine it with a little mayonnaise to create our own version of aïoli to have with soup or a fish stew. We're sure you'll find many other inventive ways of using it. Be sure to try it as a pasta sauce, but don't stop with this suggestion: use hot clam broth instead of the pasta water to thin the pesto, then add clams in their shells to the sauce. Or use bottled clam juice for thinner and add stir-fried shrimp or scallops. Instead of the shrimp or scallops, try bits of leftover fish or a drained can of solid white tuna, flaked, or canned mussels simmered in their liquid.

1 15-ounce can chickpeas, drained and rinsed

2 cups firmly packed cilantro leaves

2 large garlic cloves, coarsely chopped

¹/4 teaspoon salt or to taste

¹/4 teaspoon freshly ground pepper

¹/4 cup olive oil

In a food processor, combine the chickpeas, cilantro, garlic, salt, and pepper and pulse several times, scraping down the sides. With the motor running, add the oil in a slow, steady stream and process the mixture until smooth.

Transfer to a bowl or crock and serve with toasted pita triangles, bagel chips, crackers, or toasted thin slices of French or Italian bread.

To store for later use, pack into a container with a tight-fitting lid. The pesto will keep in the refrigerator for up to 2 weeks.

Chickpea, Cumin, and Cilantro Spiced Spread

MAKES ABOUT 3 CUPS

Serve this spread with lightly toasted ½-inch-thick rounds of French bread and your guests will forget about butter. They'll also forget about a first course—this will be it. The beans are pureed with herbs and spices and then mixed with finely chopped yellow bell pepper just before serving and sprinkled with scallions for extra flavor, texture, and color. Of course, packed into a crock or a bowl, it can find a welcome place on a buffet table surrounded by crackers, pita triangles, bagel crisps, daikon radish, and cucumber slices or whatever else you can dream up to support a daub.

In a food processor, blend everything but the bell pepper and scallions, pulsing several times and scraping down the sides, until smooth. The spread can be made to this point several days in advance and kept covered and chilled.

Just before serving, in a mixing bowl fold in the bell pepper until well combined, mound in a serving dish, and sprinkle with the scallions.

1 tablespoon fresh lemon juice

1 tablespoon white wine vinegar

1 large garlic clove, minced

1 teaspoon grated fresh ginger

½ teaspoon ground cumin or more to taste

¼ teaspoon cayenne pepper

½ teaspoon salt

¼ cup packed cilantro leaves

1 19-ounce can chickpeas, drained and rinsed

1 yellow bell pepper, seeded, deveined, and finely chopped

2 scallions, both white and green parts, very thinly sliced

Mousse of Pink Beans, Smoked Salmon, and Horseradish

This spread is wonderful on bagel crisps, slices of toasted bagel you find packaged at the supermarket. Of course, you can make your own by slicing leftover bagels in half horizontally (with the gigantic size of some bagels, you might want to slice them into thirds), placing them on a baking sheet, and baking in a preheated 350° oven until crisp and browned. For a more elegant presentation, serve the mousse with lightly toasted pumpernickel triangles, lavash, or melba toast. Use plain bagels or unflavored lavash or melba toasts as a carrier to let the flavor of the mousse predominate.

1 cup whipped regular or low-fat cream cheese

¼ pound smoked salmon, chopped

1 15-ounce can pink beans, drained and rinsed

1 tablespoon drained bottled horseradish

1 tablespoon snipped fresh dill

1 tablespoon vodka

salt to taste

½ teaspoon freshly ground pepper or more to taste

In a food processor, puree everything until the mixture is very smooth, stopping to scrape down the sides several times.

Scrape the mousse into a bowl and serve with bagel crisps or spoon into a container with a tight-fitting lid and refrigerate. The mousse can be made up to a week in advance and kept covered and chilled.

Note: The mousse can be served with finely chopped red onion on the side to sprinkle as an option.

Variation: Add 2 tablespoons chopped red onion as an option when processing the mousse.

Pink Bean Anchoïade (Provençal Anchovy-Vegetable Spread with Pink Beans)

In the south of France they love pureed spreads. Tapenade is one; this is another. Both are anchovy based, but beyond that common ingredient they are completely different. Tapenade has olives and capers; anchoïade has almonds, tomato, and red bell pepper. Neither spread is traditionally made with beans, however. Beans lend smoothness and bulk to both spreads, not to mention nutrients. Add a little chicken, beef, or vegetable broth to thin it out, and this spread turns into a marvelously zesty pasta sauce.

In a food processor, finely grind the almonds with the anchovies and garlic. With the motor running, add the shallot, oil, vinegar, and herbes de Provence and blend well. Add the beans, tomato, red bell pepper, black pepper, and parsley leaves and pulse, scraping down the sides once or twice, until the puree is smooth.

Serve at room temperature with crackers, croustades (French bread toasts), or toasted pita triangles.

$^1/_3$ cup blanched whole almonds

1 2-ounce can flat anchovies, drained and patted dry

3 large garlic cloves, quartered

1 shallot, quartered

3 tablespoons olive oil

1 tablespoon red wine vinegar

1 teaspoon herbes de Provence or dried Italian seasoning

1 15-ounce can pink beans

1 ripe tomato, seeded and chopped (about $^3/_4$ cup)

1 red bell pepper, seeded, deveined, and chopped (about $^3/_4$ cup)

$^1/_2$ teaspoon freshly ground pepper

$^1/_2$ cup finely chopped parsley leaves

Pinto Bean, Fresh Corn, and Herb Spread

MAKES ABOUT 2½ CUPS

Southwestern ingredients combine here to make a savory spread. We suggest cooked fresh corn cut right from the cob, but you can substitute frozen corn or canned corn niblets well drained when corn is not in season. In a spread as well seasoned as this one is, the difference in flavor is not crucial. We've also served this as a cold soup by adding 2 cups or so of chicken broth to the bean/corn mixture and passing the result through a sieve to remove the solids before blending it with double the amount of yogurt. The spread benefits from the bits of texture; the soup does not.

2 cups cooked fresh corn kernels or 1 10-ounce package frozen, thawed and cooked, or 1 11-ounce can, drained well

1 15-ounce can pinto beans, drained and rinsed

2 scallions, both white and green parts, thinly sliced

½ teaspoon dried thyme

½ teaspoon chili powder

½ cup low-fat or nonfat plain yogurt

2 tablespoons minced cilantro leaves

salt and freshly ground pepper to taste

In a blender or food processor, blend the corn, beans, scallions, thyme, chili powder, and yogurt, pulsing and scraping down the sides, until the mixture is very smooth.

Transfer to a serving bowl, stir in the cilantro, and season with salt and pepper.

Serve with crackers, croustades (French bread toasts), or toasted pita triangles—or thin with more yogurt until it reaches the desired consistency and serve as a dip with crudités or tortilla chips.

Pinto Bean, Carrot, Scallion, and Coriander Puree

This combination always seems to encourage diners to guess what the ingredients are. The carrots and beans are easy, but the cooked scallions and the ground coriander are a tough call. Ground coriander tastes nothing like the fresh leaves, usually sold as cilantro. And cooked scallions are rare enough in our cuisine to make them complete strangers to most diners. We think you'll agree that the blend of all four ingredients, strangers or not, is felicitous as well as surprising.

In a saucepan over moderately high heat, combine the carrots, scallions, coriander, sugar, salt, and pepper with the water. Bring the water to a boil and cook the mixture, covered, for 20 minutes or until the carrots are very tender.

Strain the mixture in a sieve, reserving the cooking liquid. Puree the carrot mixture along with the beans in a food processor until very smooth, adding enough of the reserved cooking liquid to obtain the desired consistency.

Transfer the puree to the pan set over moderately low heat and stir in the butter and more salt and pepper to taste.

Reheat the puree, stirring constantly, until it is hot. Serve immediately to spread on warm toast triangles; 2-inch lengths of baguette, split and toasted; as a dip for blanched vegetables; to fill endive leaves; or as a sauce for pasta. This puree is a perfect foil for chunks of steamed Indian flat bread.

1½ pounds carrots, scraped and thinly sliced

10 scallions, both white and green parts, cut into 1-inch lengths

1 tablespoon ground coriander

1 teaspoon sugar

1 teaspoon salt or to taste

½ teaspoon freshly ground pepper

3 cups water

1 15-ounce can pinto beans, drained and rinsed

½ stick (¼ cup) unsalted butter, cut into pieces

Red Bean, Sardine, Horseradish, and Parsley Pâté

Parsley, sardines, and red beans give this spread a fresh taste, appetizing color, and smooth consistency. The horseradish gives taste buds the kind of jolt that makes the spread a perfect companion to drinks. Just a tiny bite fills the mouth with formidable flavor. That flavor will last for a while, too. Packed into an airtight container and chilled, the pâté will keep for a week or more.

1 15-ounce can red beans, drained and rinsed

2 (3.75- to 4.75-ounce) cans skinless and boneless sardines with their oil

2 tablespoons drained bottled horseradish or to taste

1/2 cup firmly packed fresh flat-leaf parsley leaves

1 small red onion, coarsely chopped

1 teaspoon Worcestershire sauce

1 tablespoon fresh lemon juice

2 dashes Tabasco sauce or more to taste

1/2 teaspoon salt or to taste

1/2 teaspoon freshly ground pepper

In a food processor, process everything, stopping several times to scrape down the sides, until the mixture is a smooth puree. Taste for seasoning and texture. If it's too thick, add a little olive oil and process for a few seconds to combine it well.

Transfer to a serving bowl or plate surrounded with lightly toasted pita triangles, crackers, or $3/16$-inch-thick slices of cucumber or daikon radish for spreading.

White Bean and Celeriac Rémoulade Spread

MAKES ABOUT 3 CUPS

Celeriac, or celery root, is an underutilized vegetable in this country, but in rémoulade sauce as a cold salad it is almost always present on a plate of hors-d'oeuvre varié *in France. In the raw, celeriac's looks are nothing to write home about: knurled, bumpy, often brown and forbidding. But once peeled, the flesh is creamy white and the texture just short of crunchy. We love it in soups, combined with mashed potatoes, pureed, and in pancake form. Celeriac has a tendency to darken when it is pared, though, so it is best to drop it into acidulated water (water with a few drops of lemon juice or vinegar added) until you are ready to use it. Pureed raw with the other ingredients in this recipe, it transforms into a delightful spread or dip. Add some milk or cream to thin it out, and you've invented a unique cold soup.*

Peel the celeriac with a sharp knife or swivel-blade vegetable peeler. Cut it in half through the root and remove any spongy areas if necessary. Cut each half into 1/2-inch slices, stack several slices together, and cut them into 1/2-inch logs, then cut the logs into 1/2-inch dice.

Combine the celeriac with the rest of the ingredients in a food processor and puree, stopping often to scrape down the sides, until very smooth. Taste for seasoning and add more pepper, mustard, or anchovy paste if you like.

Serve the spread with toast triangles, crackers, slices of baguette, pita, or chips.

Any leftover spread can be kept, chilled in the refrigerator, for at least a week in a container with a tight-fitting lid. The spread also freezes well for about 6 weeks.

1 pound celeriac (1 large root)

1 15-ounce can small white beans, drained and rinsed

1 cup homemade or good-quality bottled mayonnaise

1 tablespoon fresh lemon juice

1 tablespoon Dijon mustard

2 tablespoons coarsely chopped sour gherkins

2 tablespoons drained bottled capers

2 tablespoons chopped fresh parsley

2 tablespoons chopped chives or scallions

2 tablespoons chopped fresh tarragon

1 tablespoon anchovy paste

1 teaspoon freshly ground pepper

Yellow Split Pea and
Yogurt Spread with Cilantro Chutney

There is an Indian snack made from yellow split peas and hot chili powder that we are addicted to. It's sold in almost every Indian food store. The brand we like best is made by Deep Foods and is called Proteedal—little half beads of peas fried to a wonderful crunchiness and seasoned with hot chili powder and salt. Yellow split peas have a nutty flavor that is perfect with hot chilies and cilantro, which is why we combined these ingredients in a spread that's sensational on sandwiches and the perfect accompaniment to poached or grilled fish fillets. Of course it can be used alone to spread on toasted baguette slices or pita triangles or pieces of steaming Indian flat bread.

1 cup dried yellow split peas

¹/₂ cup regular or low-fat
plain yogurt

1 tablespoon fresh lemon
juice

3 tablespoons cilantro chutney (recipe follows) or
more to taste

1 teaspoon salt or to taste

In a small saucepan over moderate heat, cover the split peas with water and bring to a boil, reduce the heat to simmer, and cook, covered, for 25 minutes. Drain in a colander and run under cold water.

Drain again and transfer to a food processor along with the other ingredients and process until smooth.

Cilantro Chutney

This is a wonderful Indian condiment that can be used in endless ways. It can be bought bottled in Indian and some Asian food shops and keeps well in an airtight container in the refrigerator for weeks at a time. But why not make your own?

In a small skillet over moderately low heat, toast the cumin seeds, stirring, until lightly browned and fragrant, about 1 minute. Transfer the seeds to a spice grinder or mortar and grind to a fine powder.

In a blender or food processor, combine everything and process until smooth. Spoon the chutney into a glass jar with a tight-fitting lid and refrigerate until ready to use.

1 teaspoon cumin seeds

$1^1/_2$ cups firmly packed cilantro leaves

1 small onion, finely chopped

1 large garlic clove, coarsely chopped

1 teaspoon grated fresh ginger

$1^1/_2$ teaspoons sugar

1 large fresh jalapeño or long green chili or more to taste, seeded, deveined (wear rubber gloves), and finely chopped

2 tablespoons fresh lemon juice

3 tablespoons water

$^1/_2$ teaspoon salt or to taste

White Bean, Green Olive, and Coriander Spread

Coriander seeds give this spread an interesting flavor—sort of Greek, according to our taste buds. The green olives, fresh lemon juice, and garlic further the Mediterranean connection. This spread is especially good on cheese sandwiches, but its lively, refreshing flavor also works with a basket of dinner rolls or dabbed on plain steamed vegetables as a tangy alternative to fat-based toppings. We have not added salt because green olives are usually salty enough, but add some if you wish after the mixture is pureed.

1 tablespoon coriander seeds

2 cups green olives (1 9^1/$_2$-ounce jar), rinsed and pitted

2 large garlic cloves, chopped

1 large fresh jalapeño or other green chili, seeded, deveined (wear rubber gloves), and chopped

3 tablespoons fresh lemon juice

1 tablespoon olive oil

^{1}/$_2$ teaspoon freshly ground pepper

1 15-ounce can white beans, drained and rinsed

In a food processor or blender, grind the coriander seeds until they are coarse and add the remaining ingredients. Puree the mixture, pulsing, stopping occasionally to scrape down the sides, until quite smooth. Taste for seasoning and add salt if desired.

Serve at room temperature. To store, pack into a container with a tight-fitting lid and chill. The spread can be made up to 5 days in advance and refrigerated. Bring to room temperature before serving.

HAVING FUN WITH BREAD SPREADS

Here are some off-the-cuff ideas for things to do with bread spreads that are so simple you don't need an actual recipe. These spreads are so versatile we're sure you'll find your own favorite ways to use them.

Bread spreads stay fresh tasting in a tightly covered container for up to 2 weeks in the refrigerator. If they seem a little dry or thick, mix in a tiny bit of water, adding more until you reach the spreadable consistency you like. They can also be frozen and will keep for several months if well sealed.

MASHED INTO POTATOES
Add an unexpected depth of flavor to baked or mashed potatoes by topping them with a bread spread or mashing them right in—you won't need butter or sour cream. You might want to mix the spread first with a little low-fat yogurt.

DRESSED-UP DRESSINGS
Mix a spoonful into your basic vinaigrette recipe to vary the flavor accent you splash on favorite salad greens. Or stir some into mayonnaise or yogurt to dress chicken, tuna, or shrimp salad.

JUMBLED EGGS
If you like scrambled eggs, you'll love them jumbled—blend a couple of tablespoons of bread spread into the beaten eggs. Or use them as zesty fillings for omelets. Or mash them with a little mayo into hard-cooked egg yolks when you're making deviled eggs.

THE WELL-SPREAD LOAF
When you put together your favorite meat loaf, try folding in several dollops of an appropriate bread spread to add extra flavor.

BURGER BRIGHTENER
Grill hamburgers with an appropriate bread spread laced right into the meat mixture or slathered on the bun.

UNCOMMON QUICHE

Put some zest into your next quiche by whisking a good helping of a bread spread into the egg/cheese mixture. Or spread some on the partially baked crust before pouring in the filling.

MORE SAVORY SOUPS

Before pouring the same old hot vegetable or minestrone soup into a tureen, place a couple of tablespoons of your choice of bread spread in the bottom of the tureen for a new and unusually piquant flavor addition—in other words, use it as pesto.

BETTER BREAD

Spike a bread recipe with bread spreads. Try a few tablespoons right in the batter and end up with a more fragrant, spicier, memorable loaf. Or you can roll some inside pizza dough and bake it in a preheated 425° oven for 25 to 30 minutes or until the crust is browned; serve the roll hot in thin slices. Or combine black bean tapenade with tuna (see the first recipe in this chapter) and chopped tomatoes, spread on pizza dough, top with shredded mozzarella, and you've got a Provençal Pizza.

STURDIER STEWS

Stews often need thickening. Instead of flour or cornstarch, use a nicely seasoned bean puree like our bread spreads. Mix in as much as you need to thicken the gravy and intensify the flavor.

FILLING FOR OTHER FOODS

Fill mushroom caps with bread spreads and broil for a new take on hors d'oeuvres. Fill scooped-out cherry tomatoes with ¼ teaspoon mayonnaise and a demitasse spoonful of bread spread. Do the same with cooked and cooled hollowed-out tiny new unpeeled Bliss potatoes. These one-bite savory finger foods are great with drinks.

CHEESE SPREADS

Mash a quantity of a favorite bread spread with cream cheese, softened cheddar, or other cheese. Slather on coarse black bread or rye before assembling a new-style sandwich.

FILLING FOR FROZEN PHYLLO

Make hot hors d'oeuvres: dot thawed frozen phyllo dough 2 inches apart with a teaspoonful of one of our bread spreads. Using a knife or pastry wheel, cut the dough into squares, fold each square into a little triangle, then bake at 400° until golden, about 30 minutes.

PUFF PASTE STRAWS

Thinly spread a bread spread on a sheet of thawed frozen puff paste, sprinkle with Parmesan, then top with a second sheet of dough. Cut the filled dough into $1/2$-inch strips, twist the strips a couple of times, and bake into newfangled straws at 400° for about 20 to 25 minutes.

OMELETS AND CREPES

A minute or two before an omelet is cooked to your liking and ready to be folded, tuck in a tablespoon or more of a savory bread spread (thinned, if necessary, with water, broth, or yogurt) to warm and add liveliness and intrigue. Do the same with crepes before baking in the oven under a creamy sauce.

LIVELY RICE AND POLENTA

Plain boiled or steamed rice takes on a delicious new dimension with a spicy bread spread folded in. Make a quick sauce of a thinned bread spread and spoon it over polenta for an immensely satisfying side dish.

FINESSE FOR SHRIMP OR SCALLOPS

Stir-fry a mess of shelled shrimp or scallops for a few seconds, just until they're opaque. Off the heat, toss with a good measure of an appropriate bread spread until the shellfish are well coated, then serve—all in less than 2 minutes. Finally, fast food with finesse!

HOW TO TURN BEAN SPREADS, PASTES, PÂTÉS, AND PUREES INTO PASTA SAUCES AND DIPS

It's easy to turn any one of our bread spreads into a sauce for pasta. Dips are even quicker and just as uncomplicated.

If you love pasta and want something different and delicious to serve instead of the standard sauces, try transforming a favorite bread spread into a topping for a variety of pasta shapes.

All it takes to turn a spreadable paste into a sauce is the simple addition of some of the hot pasta water to thin it. But once you've tried this, you'll have the confidence to play with the theory, using other hot liquids, changing and adding ingredients and methods to suit your tastes.

CHOOSING THE RIGHT PASTA

Enter a supermarket, specialty food store, or Italian salumeria, and you are confronted with an often bewildering display of pastas short and fat, long and thin, and everything in between, including the most imaginative shapes, both fresh and dried, in various colors and flavors.

Certain pastas are better vehicles for a particular sauce than others. If a sauce is light, you might want to choose a more delicate pasta; if it's thicker and more robust, use broader, wider noodles.

Sauces made from bread spreads start out with a puree of ingredients that are thinned with a liquid. They are usually not chunky. So they may go best with shapes that can hold some of the sauce, such as shells, penne, rigatoni, rotelle, lumache, or bow ties. Just use logic and your own particular inclination and preference.

PASTA SAUCE. For every pound of dried pasta, serving four, stir together in a serving or mixing bowl $^3/_4$ cup bread spread along with $^2/_3$ cup hot pasta cooking water to thin it. When the pasta has been cooked al dente, drain it in a colander, add it to the thinned spread mixture, and toss well to combine. Often the mixture gains in flavor if you add the juice of $^1/_2$ lemon and salt and pepper to taste.

THE 60-SECOND TRANSFORMATION
FROM BREAD SPREAD TO DIP

It takes only a minute to turn a bread spread into a savory dip to serve with crackers, potato chips, toasted pita triangles, bagel chips, tortilla chips, thin slices of cocktail rye or pumpernickel, toasted slices of French or Italian bread, or bite-size pieces of raw or blanched fresh, crunchy vegetables.

DIPS. To each 2 cups bread spread, add ½ cup homemade or good-quality bottled mayonnaise, sour cream, or plain yogurt and combine the mixture well in a bowl, blender, or food processor. For a creamier, thinner dip, increase the amount of mayonnaise, sour cream, or yogurt, or add milk, cream, broth, tomato juice, clam juice, or any suitable liquid. Transfer to a serving bowl and surround with the dipping vehicle of your choice.

SOUPS

ICE BOX SOUPS

Like Spanish gazpacho, ice box soups are really pureed salads. They are late spring and summer soups, to serve when you'd rather not turn on the stove. All the ingredients come straight from the refrigerator and the pantry shelf and are popped into the food processor, whirled into a smooth puree, then ladled into soup bowls—from scratch to mouth almost as fast as it takes to explain them.

Ice box soups are also quite versatile. Once they are pureed and blended, you can transform them into winter meal starters by pouring them into a saucepan and heating, stirring occasionally, for 10 minutes.

Garden-Fresh Black Bean Salsa Soup

SERVES 4 TO 6

Just what is a fresh salsa? In Mexico it usually consists of fresh tomatoes or tomatillos and/or bell peppers, chopped onion, chopped cilantro leaves, minced chilies, perhaps some lime juice, a touch of garlic, and whatever else the cook has on hand that might lend a personal touch. All these fresh vegetables are a great base for an unusual black bean soup with a mouth-tingling zest and freshness. This uncooked soup is definitely worth adding to your repertoire—it's one of the most seductive summer soups around. Just whirl it in your food processor or blender and garnish the puree with some chopped scallions or cilantro leaves (perhaps, sprinkled on a dollop of sour cream).

1 15-ounce can black bean soup

3 red ripe tomatoes, peeled, seeded, and cut into $1/2$-inch dice

1 red bell pepper, seeded, deveined, and cut into $1/2$-inch dice

2 jalapeño chilies, seeded, deveined (wear rubber gloves), and minced

1 large garlic clove, minced

1 large sweet onion, finely chopped

$1/4$ cup firmly packed chopped cilantro leaves

$1/4$ cup fresh lime juice

salt and freshly ground pepper to taste

In a large bowl, combine all the ingredients and let the mixture stand at room temperature for at least 15 minutes, stirring occasionally, so that the flavors mellow and some juices are formed. The soup will keep, covered tightly and chilled, for several days.

Note: The soup can be served chunky or pureed in a processor or blender to desired consistency. For a thinner soup, add cold tomato juice, cold chicken broth, or water.

Curried Ice Box Soup with Cilantro Chutney

We love cold soups that sting the tongue. This one gets its sting from the cilantro chutney. The soup itself is somewhat sweet from the combination of curry and bell pepper, somewhat sour from the buttermilk and lemon juice. It takes no time to make and is completely refreshing on a warm evening. Fill a thermos with it and take the ice-cold soup along on a summer picnic in the country or at the beach.

In a food processor or blender, puree everything but the buttermilk and basil until very smooth. Add the buttermilk and pulse the mixture until just combined.

Chill the soup (it can be made up to 3 days in advance) further if you like and serve very cold garnished with the basil.

1 19-ounce can chickpeas, drained and rinsed

1 red bell pepper, seeded, deveined, and chopped

1 large garlic clove, minced

1 medium onion, minced or grated

1 cup chilled chicken broth

1 teaspoon curry powder or garam masala

1 tablespoon fresh lemon juice or to taste

1 tablespoon cilantro chutney (page 75)

$1/4$ teaspoon sugar

1 cup buttermilk

2 teaspoons finely chopped fresh basil leaves for garnish

Lima Bean, Cucumber, and Toasted Cumin Buttermilk Ice Box Soup

SERVES 4

If you puree the lima beans in this recipe while they are still frozen in a block (break off chunks just small enough to fit into the bowl of a food processor), there's no need to chill this soup. And if the cucumbers have been refrigerated, so much the better. When all the ingredients are at hand and have been chilled—but not the garlic or the cumin—you can have this surprisingly thirst-quenching soup on the table in less than 10 minutes. Garnish with the thinnest possible slices of cucumber and a sprinkling of chopped chives or parsley, and you have an elegant starter.

1 10-ounce package frozen Fordhook or baby lima beans, the block broken into small chunks

4 cucumbers (about 2 pounds), peeled, seeded, and cut into small chunks, 8 paper-thin unpeeled slices reserved for garnish

$1/2$ teaspoon cumin seeds, toasted lightly in a skillet

1 large garlic clove, chopped

1 cup buttermilk

salt and freshly ground white pepper to taste

2 teaspoons chopped fresh chives or parsley leaves for garnish

In a food processor or blender, puree the frozen lima beans, cucumbers, cumin seeds, garlic, and buttermilk until the mixture is smooth.

Transfer the soup to a serving bowl, season it with salt and pepper, and garnish with the reserved cucumber slices sprinkled with the chives.

Dilled Pink Bean, Yogurt, and Shrimp Ice Box Soup

This soothing summer soup is based on one we had at a friend's dinner party, which was served on a huge screened-in porch in Southampton overlooking the pounding Atlantic surf. The original came from her mother's recipe file and was made with buttermilk. Buttermilk was easier to find in the 1940s, when her mom first transcribed this recipe, so we changed the buttermilk to low-fat yogurt, added the pink beans, and threw in some fresh dill. This new soup is prettier, tastier, and healthier. That's what we always strive for: a dish that looks good, tastes good, and is good for you. Now, if we could only provide that porch along with the recipe.

In a food processor, puree 1 cup of the yogurt with the beans, mustard, salt, pepper, and apple until the mixture is very smooth.

Transfer to a large bowl and stir in the remaining yogurt, shrimp, chopped cucumber, dill, and chives until combined well.

Serve cold, garnishing each serving with a slice of cucumber. The soup can be made ahead and chilled, covered, until it is very cold.

Note: Instead of using shrimp, you can transform this soup into something with a Greek inclination by using 1 8-ounce jar of tarama (fish roe available at Greek and Middle Eastern stores, specialty food stores, and some supermarkets). If you do, substitute the sugar for the apple. The taste of tarama is different from shrimp but completely seductive. Just remember, when mixing in the tarama, do it gently so that most of the little eggs remain whole and don't burst prematurely in the bowl. They should burst delightfully, with each spoonful, in your mouth.

- 1 quart low-fat plain yogurt, very cold, or buttermilk
- 1 15-ounce can pink beans, drained and rinsed
- 1 tablespoon dry mustard
- 1 teaspoon salt or to taste
- 1/2 teaspoon freshly ground pepper
- 1 small Delicious apple, peeled, cored, and chopped, or 1 teaspoon sugar
- 1/2 pound shrimp, cooked, peeled, chopped, and well chilled
- 1 cucumber, chilled, peeled, seeded, and finely chopped, plus cucumber slices for garnish
- 2 tablespoons snipped fresh dill
- 2 tablespoons minced fresh chives

Dilled Pinto Bean and Tomato Ice Box Soup

SERVES 6 TO 8

This is a short-order cold soup that doesn't even need refrigeration. That's because it's chilled by adding ice cubes to the blender or processor when the ingredients are pureed. The room-temperature tomatoes and beans are cooled off just enough by the ice cubes for spooning up on a warm evening. Any leftover soup can be frozen or kept covered in the refrigerator for a few days until you feel like adding some other fresh vegetables—cucumbers, garlic, radishes, spinach, lettuce, parsley, or anything else that inspires you. Just puree the newcomers with some of the tomato/bean soup, mix it back into the remaining soup, add a dollop of yogurt or sour cream, and a completely new ice box soup is born.

1 28-ounce can imported
  Italian tomatoes with their
  juice
1 15-ounce can pinto beans,
  drained and rinsed
3 scallions, both white and
  green parts, thinly sliced
juice of 1 lime
$\frac{1}{2}$ teaspoon sugar if desired
3 tablespoons minced fresh
  dill
1 cup ice cubes
salt and freshly ground
  pepper to taste

In a large bowl, combine all the ingredients, and in a blender or food processor puree the mixture in batches until very smooth. Taste for seasoning and transfer the soup to a tureen or ladle into soup bowls.

Note: The soup can be garnished any number of ways, but we like it topped with finely chopped dill pickle—or add the pickle, coarsely chopped, to the mixture before pureeing so it becomes part of the soup itself.

You can add heat to this cold soup by sprinkling in a few dashes of Tabasco sauce before pureeing or by mixing in a tablespoon of drained bottled horseradish or both.

Curried Red Bean, Carrot, and Ginger Ice Box Soup

SERVES 4 TO 6

This quick soup has the tingle of fresh ginger to recommend it along with the fragrance of curry. Turn it into a lively winter soup by simmering for a few minutes.

In a food processor, puree the onion, oil, beans, carrots, ginger, curry powder, and chutney with 1 cup of the chicken broth until very smooth.

Transfer to a large bowl or tureen and stir in the remaining chicken broth, ice water, lemon juice, salt, and pepper. The soup can be made up to 3 days in advance and kept covered and chilled.

Serve cold topped with a sprinkling of cilantro leaves and peanuts.

1 medium onion, chopped

1 tablespoon canola or peanut oil

1 15-ounce can red beans, drained and rinsed

6 carrots (about 1¼ pounds), peeled and coarsely chopped

1 2-inch piece of fresh ginger, peeled and coarsely chopped

1 teaspoon curry powder

1 tablespoon Major Grey's chutney, finely chopped

2 cups cold chicken broth, skimmed of any fat

2 cups ice water

1 tablespoon fresh lemon juice or to taste

salt and freshly ground white pepper to taste

2 tablespoons minced cilantro leaves

2 tablespoons minced dry-roasted peanuts

White Bean, Cucumber, Basil, and Yogurt Ice Box Soup

You make this soup with very cold ingredients straight from the refrigerator combined right in the serving tureen. Of course, the soup can be made ahead and chilled. But don't make it too far ahead; the fresh flavors of the vegetables should be retained.

4 Kirby cucumbers (about $^1/_2$ pound), peeled, seeded, and coarsely grated

1 15-ounce can white beans, drained, rinsed, and coarsely mashed with a fork or potato masher

1 cup plain yogurt

1 cup milk

$^1/_4$ cup half-and-half

$^1/_4$ cup firmly packed minced fresh basil leaves

4 scallions, both white and green parts, finely chopped

1 small garlic clove, minced

2 teaspoons tarragon vinegar

salt and freshly ground white pepper to taste

In a serving bowl or tureen, combine all the ingredients, stir well, and serve.

Note: To cut calories and fat, use low-fat or nonfat yogurt and $1^1/_4$ cups 1% low-fat milk instead of the whole milk and half-and-half.

Black Bean and Meatball Soup

SERVES 6

We love black beans, especially in black bean soup. We often use canned black bean soup, undiluted, as a sauce for a side dish of rice when we're really in a hurry. Here we liven it up a bit with tiny meatballs and a sprinkling of fresh garlic. Serve this over rice and you have a substantial one-dish meal. Add a small arugula salad.

In a stainless-steel mixing bowl, combine the ground beef, bread crumbs, Parmesan, 1 teaspoon salt, pepper, and cayenne and mix thoroughly. With a demitasse spoon or $1/2$-teaspoon measure, form tiny meatballs.

In a large sauté pan over high heat, heat the oil to rippling. Brown the meatballs in the oil, shaking the pan often and stirring occasionally, until the meatballs are firm and nicely colored, about 5 minutes. Remove the meatballs with a slotted spoon and set them aside. In the oil remaining in the pan sauté the carrot, celery, and onions, stirring occasionally, until they are softened, about 5 minutes.

Add the tomato sauce, lower the heat to moderate, and simmer for 5 minutes. Add the boiling water and remaining salt, stir in the reserved meatballs and the black bean soup, cover, and simmer for 5 minutes more.

Remove the pan from the heat and stir in the garlic and cilantro. Taste for seasoning and serve hot.

1 pound lean ground beef

2 tablespoons fresh bread crumbs

1 tablespoon grated Parmesan cheese (if desired)

2 teaspoons salt

$1/2$ teaspoon freshly ground pepper

pinch of cayenne pepper

2 tablespoons olive oil

1 large carrot, peeled and cut into $1/4$-inch dice

1 celery rib with leaves, cut into $1/4$-inch dice

2 medium onions, finely chopped

1 8-ounce can tomato sauce

2 cups boiling water

2 15-ounce cans black bean soup

1 large garlic clove, minced

$1/3$ cup chopped cilantro or flat-leaf parsley

Gingered Black-Eyed Pea and Parsnip Soup

SERVES 4

We often turn to parsnips for their soothing sweetness—especially in a comforting, chill-erasing hot soup. Parsnips are underused (once a leading contender, they were deposed by the newly discovered potato in the centuries following the European invasion of the New World). So are black-eyed peas. Together they make a delightfully earthy soup evocative of parsley, nuts, and radishes—although none of these ingredients are in this concoction—with a particularly fresh aroma.

2 tablespoons unsalted butter or canola oil

1 medium onion, finely chopped

2 large garlic cloves, minced

1 tablespoon minced fresh ginger

1 medium carrot, thinly sliced

1 celery rib, thinly sliced

6 parsnips (about 1½ pounds), peeled and cut into ½-inch dice

1 quart chicken broth

1 15-ounce can black-eyed peas, drained and rinsed

½ teaspoon freshly grated nutmeg or more to taste

salt and freshly ground pepper to taste

In a heavy saucepan or soup kettle over moderately low heat, bring the butter to foaming. When the foam subsides, cook the onion, garlic, ginger, carrot, and celery, stirring, until the onion is softened, about 5 minutes. Add the parsnips and broth, turn the heat up to high, and bring the liquid to a boil. Reduce the heat to simmer and cook the mixture, covered, for 15 minutes or until the vegetables are tender.

Stir in the black-eyed peas, nutmeg, salt, and pepper and heat through for 5 minutes more. Serve hot.

Note: Both black-eyed peas and parsnips are silky smooth when pureed, so the soup's chunky texture can be smoothed in a blender or food processor to serve the soup cold during the summer. Whisk in a cup of plain yogurt just before serving.

Chickpea, Chicken, and Chipotle Chili Soup

SERVES 8

The chipotle chilies we use in this soup come canned in adobo sauce and are available at Hispanic markets and at some enlightened specialty food shops and supermarkets. What is amazing is that a soup so robust and filling can be made so quickly. In Mexico soups like this usually require a good deal of preparation and long simmering. This one achieves the same rich combination of flavors in about 20 minutes.

In a large saucepan or soup kettle over moderately high heat, bring the oil to rippling and in it cook the onion, stirring, until it is softened, about 3 to 5 minutes. Add the garlic and cook, stirring, for 1 minute more. Add the carrots, zucchini, and cabbage and cook, stirring, for 1 minute.

Stir in the broth and chickpeas, bring the mixture to a boil, reduce heat to simmer, and cook for 8 minutes, or until the carrots are just tender.

Stir the chicken into the soup along with the chilies and cook for another 5 minutes or until the chicken is poached.

Add salt and pepper and, just before serving, stir in the cilantro. Garnish each soup bowl with a lime wedge.

Note: Turn this soup into a rugged one-dish meal by enriching it further with extra chicken or some cooked sausage slices, diced leftover pork roast, or what have you.

1½ tablespoons vegetable oil

1 medium onion, halved lengthwise and thinly sliced

2 large garlic cloves, minced

2 carrots, halved lengthwise and cut into ⅛-inch slices

1 zucchini, halved lengthwise and cut into ¼-inch slices

½ small head of cabbage (about ¾ pound), shredded

2 quarts chicken broth

1 19-ounce can chickpeas, drained and rinsed

1 large whole skinless, boneless chicken breast, cut into bite-size pieces

2 drained canned whole chipotle chilies in adobo, rinsed, seeded, deveined (wear rubber gloves), and cut into tiny dice

salt and freshly ground pepper to taste

½ cup minced fresh cilantro leaves

lime wedges for garnish

Moroccan-Style Chickpea, Chicken, and Lentil Soup

SERVES 6 TO 8

Harira is what the Moroccans call this soup, and it's often made with lamb as well as chicken. Our version uses boned chicken breasts to speed up the cooking time and to lower the fat content. It's just as delicious, however. The seasonings are just salt and pepper, which allow the flavors of the ingredients to take over, melding quickly into a savory, hearty brew. To turn this into a one-dish meal, allow a boned chicken breast half, not diced, for each diner and increase the cooking time by 5 minutes.

6 cups chicken broth

1 28- to 32-ounce can whole tomatoes, coarsely chopped, with their juice

$1/4$ teaspoon crumbled saffron threads or $1/4$ teaspoon ground turmeric

2 medium onions, finely chopped

1 19-ounce can chickpeas, drained and rinsed

$1/2$ cup long-grain white rice

$1/2$ cup lentils

1 whole skinless, boneless chicken breast, cut into $1/2$-inch dice

1 teaspoon salt or to taste

$1/2$ teaspoon freshly ground pepper or to taste

1 cup finely chopped cilantro leaves

1 cup finely chopped fresh parsley leaves

In a large soup kettle or saucepan over moderately high heat, bring the broth to a boil. Add the tomatoes, saffron, onions, chickpeas, rice, and lentils, return to a boil, reduce the heat to simmer, and cook, covered, for 15 minutes.

Add the diced chicken, salt, and pepper and cook, covered, for 10 minutes more or until the flavors blend, the chicken is cooked through, and the lentils are tender.

Just before serving, stir in the cilantro and parsley.

Chickpea and Cod Soup with Pickled Pepper Garnish

SERVES 4 GENEROUSLY

Beans turn the trick here: they add texture and absorb the other flavors, including the fish, quickly and handily. They supply so much substance, in fact, that this soup could serve as a one-dish meal.

In a soup pot or kettle over moderately high heat, bring the oil to rippling and in it sauté the onion, bell pepper, cabbage, and celery, stirring, until the vegetables are soft but not browned, about 8 minutes.

Stir in the paprika, salt, and pepper and place the fish in one layer over the vegetables. Add the clam juice, water, and wine and bring the liquid just to a boil. Reduce the heat to simmer and cook the mixture, partially covered, for 10 minutes or until the fish just flakes. Gently stir in the chickpeas.

In a small bowl, whisk together the yolks, flour, and $^1/_2$ cup of the sour cream, whisk about 1 cup of the soup broth into the mixture in a stream, and when completely blended stir the mixture back into the soup. Don't worry if some of the fish flakes and breaks apart when stirring.

Taste for seasoning, reduce the heat to moderately low, and simmer (do not allow to boil or the sour cream will curdle) for 5 minutes more, uncovered.

Ladle into 4 bowls, dividing the fish equally, and garnish each serving with a dollop of the remaining sour cream and a teaspoon of the hot peppers.

2 tablespoons olive, canola, or vegetable oil

1 medium onion, finely chopped

1 red bell pepper, seeded, deveined, and finely chopped

2 cups finely shredded cabbage

1 celery rib with leaves, finely chopped

1 tablespoon sweet paprika

$^1/_2$ teaspoon salt or to taste

$^1/_2$ teaspoon freshly ground pepper

$1^1/_2$ pounds cod fillet, cut into 2-inch pieces

1 cup bottled clam juice combined with 1 cup water

1 cup dry white wine

1 15-ounce can chickpeas, drained and rinsed

2 large egg yolks

$^1/_4$ cup all-purpose flour

$^3/_4$ cup sour cream or plain yogurt

4 teaspoons finely chopped pickled jalapeño chili or hot cherry peppers

Curried Chickpea Bisque

We love Indian food and predict that it will be the next ethnic culinary wave to sweep the country. This soup tastes Indian but has never been within 5,000 miles of the Taj Mahal. It's our version of some vegetarian dishes we've eaten in Indian restaurants in New York City turned into a bisque—a thick pureed soup combined with cream. We use yogurt here instead of cream because it's more Indian and because it seems to heighten flavors rather than mask them. Nonfat or low-fat yogurt may be used.

$1/2$ stick ($1/4$ cup) unsalted butter

1 large yellow onion, coarsely chopped

1 unpeeled cucumber, seeded and chopped

$1/2$ cup finely chopped cilantro leaves

1 large boiling potato (about $1/2$ pound), peeled and cut into $1/2$-inch dice

1 19-ounce can chickpeas, drained and rinsed

2 teaspoons curry powder or garam masala

$1/2$ teaspoon salt

$1/4$ teaspoon cayenne pepper or more to taste

2 cups chicken broth

2 cups plain yogurt

2 scallions, both white and green parts, thinly sliced on a diagonal

In a kettle over moderate heat, melt the butter. When the foam subsides, cook the onion, cucumber, cilantro, potato, and chickpeas in it, stirring occasionally, for 15 minutes. Stir in the curry powder, salt, and cayenne and cook for 30 seconds more.

Remove the kettle from the heat and in a food processor or blender puree the vegetable mixture with the broth in batches.

Return the puree to the kettle over moderately low heat and simmer, stirring frequently, for 10 minutes. Stir in the yogurt and continue to simmer until heated through, about 2 minutes.

Ladle the bisque into soup bowls and garnish each serving with some of the scallions.

Chilled Fava Bean Soup with Basil

Pesto isn't the only thing to make with an overabundance of basil—either from a kitchen garden or those enormous bunches offered at green markets during the season. This emerald-green sparkling soup uses up the remains of a big bunch of basil—4 cups of leaves. The puree, without the yogurt addition, freezes well. Add the yogurt after the soup has barely defrosted and serve the soup chilled. Out of basil season, the defrosted soup can be garnished with a lemon slice, chopped scallions, or radishes.

In a large saucepan over moderately high heat, melt the butter. When the foam subsides, add the onions and cook, stirring, until the onions are transparent, about 5 minutes. Add the 4 cups basil leaves and stir just until the leaves are wilted, about 2 minutes.

Add the chicken broth and bring to a boil. Reduce the heat to simmer, add the beans, and cook for 5 minutes more.

In a food processor or blender, puree the soup in batches until smooth. Chill in the freezer for 10 minutes, then stir in the yogurt, salt, and pepper. Ladle into soup bowls and garnish each bowl with the remaining basil leaves.

2 tablespoons unsalted butter

1 medium onion, chopped

4 cups fresh basil leaves plus additional leaves for garnish

6 cups chicken broth

1 15-ounce can fava or white beans, drained and rinsed

1 cup low-fat or nonfat plain yogurt

salt and freshly ground pepper to taste

Garden Soup with Eight Greens and a Hint of Curry

SERVES 4 TO 6

Led by green beans, seven other fresh green vegetables give this soup not only its intensely green color but an equally green flavor evocative of a country farm stand. It takes only 20 minutes to cook, which also ensures a fresh taste, and is made from vegetables always readily available at your local greengrocer—joined together in delicious harmony by the curry and yogurt. We usually garnish the pureed soup with chopped cucumber for crunch, but you can also use dill sprigs, cilantro leaves for additional flavor or a spiral of red or yellow bell pepper puree for color contrast.

3 cups chicken broth

3 cups coarsely chopped green beans

1 cup chopped fresh parsley

1 cup firmly packed chopped spinach leaves

1 cup firmly packed chopped watercress

1/2 cup sliced scallions, both white and green parts

2 cups finely chopped celery, including leaves

1 unpeeled medium cucumber (preferably Kirby), chopped

1/3 cup seeded, deveined, and chopped green bell pepper

3 cups chopped broccoli, including stems

salt and freshly ground pepper to taste

1 cup low-fat or nonfat plain yogurt or half-and-half

1/2 teaspoon curry powder

In a large saucepan over moderate heat, bring the broth, green beans, parsley, spinach, watercress, scallions, celery, half the cucumber, and the green bell pepper to a simmer and cook, stirring occasionally, for 10 minutes. Add the broccoli and continue to cook for 10 minutes or until all the vegetables are tender. Season with salt and pepper.

In a blender or food processor, puree the soup in batches. Return to a clean saucepan over moderately low heat, stir in the yogurt and curry powder, and heat the soup for 2 minutes more.

Ladle into warm soup bowls and garnish with the remaining chopped cucumber.

Soothing Lentil, Sausage, and Basmati Rice Soup

This thick and hearty comfort soup takes only 30 minutes to get to the table—yet it's as robust as any that sits on the back burner for hours at a time. Its aroma perfumes the house and suggests lots of effort has been going on in the kitchen.

In a soup kettle or large saucepan over high heat, combine everything but the cilantro and vinegar and bring to a boil. Reduce the heat to simmer and cook, covered, stirring occasionally, for 20 to 25 minutes or until the lentils are tender but not falling apart.

Stir in the cilantro and vinegar and taste for seasoning, adding more salt and pepper if necessary. The soup will be thick and will thicken even further as it stands. Thin it, if you like, with more hot broth or water. Ladle into warm soup bowls and serve.

5 cups chicken broth

3 cups water

1 1/2 cups lentils

1 cup white or brown basmati rice

1 pound kielbasa, cut into 1/4-inch slices

1 35-ounce can whole tomatoes, drained and chopped, the juice reserved

2 carrots, quartered lengthwise and cut into 1/4-inch pieces

1 medium onion, finely chopped

2 celery ribs with leaves, finely chopped

4 large garlic cloves, minced

1/2 teaspoon ground coriander

1/2 teaspoon ground cumin

1/2 teaspoon ground cardamom

1/8 teaspoon cayenne pepper

1 teaspoon salt or to taste

freshly ground black pepper to taste

1/2 cup minced cilantro leaves

1 tablespoon sherry vinegar

Chilled Curried Pinto Bean and Gingered Carrot Soup

SERVES 4

We love the combination of carrots and ginger. In this recipe they're pureed with pinto beans to smooth things out and flavored with curry powder to produce a luxurious chilled soup. Whisk in heavy cream instead of the yogurt for more luxury—and calories.

1 tablespoon canola or vegetable oil

1 medium onion, finely chopped

1 pound carrots, quartered lengthwise and cut into $1/4$-inch pieces

2 heaped tablespoons minced fresh ginger

1 teaspoon curry powder or garam masala or more to taste

1 15-ounce can pinto beans, rinsed and drained

3 cups chicken broth

1 cup plain yogurt

2 tablespoons chopped cilantro leaves

2 scallions, both white and green parts, finely sliced

Heat the oil in a large saucepan over moderate heat. Add the onion, carrots, and ginger and cook, covered, stirring occasionally, until the onion has softened, about 3 minutes. Add the curry and cook the mixture, stirring, for 1 minute more.

Stir in the pinto beans and the broth, turn the heat to high, and bring the liquid to a boil. Turn the heat down to simmer and cook the mixture for 15 minutes or until the carrots are very tender.

In a blender or food processor, puree the soup in batches, then let it cool completely. Cover the soup and chill it until it's cold, at least 2 hours.

Just before serving, whisk in the yogurt, divide the soup among 4 soup bowls, and sprinkle with the cilantro and scallions.

Red Bean Soup with Orange and Lemon

SERVES 4 TO 6

Pureed or mashed beans lend a rich-tasting quality to soups without dairy products. Besides adding nutritious vitamins and minerals, beans subtract the calories and fat of creamed equivalents. The texture is similar but often more flavorful because cream or milk tends to subdue the flavors of other ingredients. Most creamed soups can lead a double life—they can be served hot or chilled. So can many of those made with mashed or pureed beans, such as this one. The combination of orange and lemon not only brightens the flavor of this soup but adds a shot of vitamin C as well—one of the two vitamins beans are stingy about offering (the other is vitamin A).

In a soup kettle over moderate heat, melt the butter. When the foam subsides, stir in the celery, onion, and garlic and cook until the vegetables are softened, about 5 minutes. Stir in the red beans, broth, and water, reduce the heat to simmer, and cook the mixture, partially covered, for 15 minutes or until the beans are falling apart. Add the orange and lemon juices and cook for 1 minute more.

With a potato masher, mash the beans and vegetables until the soup is a coarse puree. Stir in the parsley, salt, and pepper. Serve the soup hot or chilled.

Note: A thin slice of orange or lemon is a pretty garnish for each serving.

½ stick (¼ cup) unsalted butter or ¼ cup vegetable oil

2 cups chopped celery, including the leaves

2 cups chopped onion

2 large garlic cloves, minced

1 19-ounce can red beans, drained and rinsed

3 cups chicken broth

1 cup water

⅓ cup fresh orange juice

3 tablespoons fresh lemon juice

¼ cup minced fresh parsley or cilantro leaves

salt and freshly ground pepper to taste

Hot or Cold White Bean, Arugula, and Fennel Soup

SERVES 6 TO 8

We like soups that can be served at any time of year, soups that taste terrific hot or cold. This one is a good example. It uses the neglected fennel to good advantage and bolsters the bulb's anise flavor with fennel seeds. Barely wilted arugula lends a spicy undertone (you can substitute watercress, dandelion leaves, mustard greens, spinach, or Swiss chard if arugula isn't available), and the beans smooth it all out.

2 tablespoons olive oil

2 pounds fennel bulbs (about 2 large, without the stalks), some of the feathery fronds reserved for garnish

1 medium onion, chopped

2 cups chicken broth

2 cups water

1 teaspoon fennel seeds

1 15-ounce can white beans, drained and rinsed

salt and freshly ground pepper to taste

3/4 pound arugula (about 1 large bunch), coarse stems discarded

In a soup kettle over moderate heat, bring the oil to rippling. Add the fennel and onion, cover, and cook for 10 minutes, stirring occasionally. Add the broth, water, and fennel seeds, reduce the heat to simmer, and cook the mixture, covered, for 10 to 15 minutes more or until the fennel is tender. Stir in the beans and cook for 2 minutes or until the beans are heated through. Add salt and pepper. Stir in the arugula and cook only until wilted, about 1 minute.

In a blender or food processor, puree the soup in batches. To serve hot, return the puree to the kettle and heat briefly over moderately low heat. To serve cold, refrigerate the puree for 1/2 hour or up to 24 hours.

Ladle into soup bowls and garnish each serving with one or two fennel fronds.

White Bean and Cauliflower Soup Speckled with Bacon

SERVES 6 TO 8

The ethnic source of this soup has been lost over the years. We think it was originally made with escarole, which would peg it as Italian. The cauliflower could be an American innovation. But cilantro also gives it a Mexican, Indian, or Chinese touch. The fact that it cooks for less than 30 minutes is most likely the result of New York City urgency—and slicing the onions and potatoes really thin. But who cares about origins when the outcome is as savory, aromatic, and delicious as this soup is?

In a soup kettle over moderate heat, cook the bacon until it's crisp, about 5 to 7 minutes. Drain on paper towels and crumble. Pour off the fat from the kettle and set it back over moderate heat. Add the oil and the garlic and cook, stirring, until it begins to turn golden, about 1 minute.

Add the onion, potatoes, cilantro, cauliflower, broth, beans, and bacon, turn the heat to high, and bring to a boil. Immediately reduce the heat to simmer and cook, stirring occasionally, for 20 minutes or until the potatoes are tender. Stir in the vinegar, cayenne, salt, and pepper.

Serve very hot, sprinkling each serving with the scallions.

4 slices lean bacon

2 tablespoons olive oil

2 tablespoons minced garlic

1 large yellow onion, quartered and thinly sliced

2 boiling potatoes (about $3/4$ pound), peeled, quartered, and thinly sliced

$1/2$ cup finely chopped cilantro leaves

1 small head of cauliflower (about $1 1/2$ pounds), broken into bite-size florets

6 cups chicken broth

2 19-ounce cans cannellini, drained and rinsed

$1/4$ cup red wine vinegar

$1/4$ teaspoon cayenne pepper

salt and freshly ground pepper to taste

4 scallions, both white and green parts, thinly sliced

White Bean, Leek, and Sausage Soup

SERVES 4

This soup borrows from several cuisines. It's the kind of cooking that is becoming an American culinary signature. Our melting-pot culture has finally reached into the kitchen—bringing together the best of all worlds—not just in this soup but in most of the food we eat at home and in restaurants these days.

$^1/_2$ teaspoon cumin seeds

$^1/_2$ teaspoon caraway seeds

2 tablespoons unsalted butter

2 medium leeks, white parts only, halved lengthwise, thinly sliced crosswise, washed well, and drained (about 2$^1/_2$ cups)

1 quart chicken broth

1 15-ounce can white beans, drained, rinsed, and pureed

$^1/_2$ pound kielbasa, cut crosswise into $^1/_4$-inch slices, the slices quartered

2 tablespoons heavy cream or low-fat or nonfat plain yogurt

salt and freshly ground pepper to taste

$^1/_2$ cup thinly sliced arugula leaves, some coarse stems removed

In a heavy saucepan or sauté pan over moderate heat, toast the cumin and caraway seeds for 2 or 3 minutes, stirring constantly until they are very fragrant. Transfer them to a plate or bowl.

In the same pan, melt the butter. When the foam subsides, sauté the leeks in it, stirring occasionally, for 5 minutes or until they are very soft.

Stir in the broth, increase the heat to moderately high, and bring the mixture to a boil. Reduce the heat to simmer and cook the mixture for 10 minutes. Stir in the reserved toasted seeds, pureed beans, kielbasa, cream, salt, and pepper and cook the soup for 5 minutes more. Just before serving, stir in the arugula leaves.

White Bean and Escarole Soup

SERVES 8

Sometimes a simple soup is called for. This one is just that: very easy, very quick, yet very tasty. The beans keep it filling and add a nice texture. You can make it even more filling by doubling the amount of beans, turning the soup into a one-dish meal. A salad is always refreshing after a hearty soup—and that still leaves room for dessert.

In a kettle over moderate heat, bring the oil to rippling. Add the garlic and cook, stirring, until it is just golden, about 1 minute. Add the onion and cook, stirring, until the onion is softened, about 5 minutes.

Add the broth and oregano, increase the heat to high, and bring the mixture to a boil. Reduce the heat to simmer, add the beans, and cook for 5 minutes. Add the escarole, salt, and pepper and simmer the soup for 5 minutes more.

Ladle the soup into warmed soup bowls, garnish with the egg white, and sprinkle generously with the Parmesan.

2 tablespoons olive oil

4 large garlic cloves, minced

1 medium onion, chopped

3 quarts chicken broth

1 teaspoon dried oregano, crumbled

1 19-ounce can white beans, drained and rinsed

1 head of escarole (at least 1 pound), cut into $1/2$-inch-wide strips

salt and freshly ground pepper to taste

4 hard-cooked eggs, whites only, sliced lengthwise into $1/8$-inch julienne strips

1 cup grated Parmesan cheese

Avgolemono with White Beans and Fennel

SERVES 6

If you've never tasted fennel, try it the next time you see it at your greenmarket. If it hasn't already been guillotined, just trim off the long stalks with their beautiful feathery fronds (use them to garnish other dishes or to add flavor to a vegetable broth). Cut the bulb into ¹/₂-inch slices, drizzle with a little olive oil, shave some Parmesan over them, and serve a couple of slices to a portion as a first course or salad. The flavor and celerylike crispness will sell itself. You'll definitely want to try this Greek-style fennel/bean soup, its licorice flavor fortified with a little anise liqueur and soothed with the traditional Greek lemon–egg yolk combination.

1¹/₂ tablespoons unsalted butter

1 large fennel bulb (about 1 pound), trimmed and sliced lengthwise into thin julienne strips (about 1¹/₂ to 2 cups), plus 3 or 4 tablespoons snipped green feathery fronds for garnish

2 shallots, minced

1 tablespoon ouzo, Pernod, or other anise-flavored liqueur

6 cups chicken broth

1 15-ounce can cannellini, drained, rinsed, and pureed with a little of the chicken broth

¹/₄ cup fresh lemon juice

2 large egg yolks

In a soup kettle or large saucepan over moderately low heat, bring the butter to foaming. When the foam subsides, cook the sliced fennel and shallots, stirring occasionally, for 5 minutes.

Add the ouzo and the broth, turn the heat to high, and bring the mixture to a boil. Reduce the heat to simmer and cook the mixture, covered, for 10 minutes. Stir in the bean puree and continue cooking for 5 minutes more or until the fennel is just tender but not soft. Remove the pan from the heat.

In a heatproof bowl, whisk together the lemon juice and egg yolks and whisk into it 1 cup of the soup liquid, pouring it in a stream as you whisk.

Add the lemon/egg mixture to the kettle, whisking. Return the kettle to moderately low heat and heat the soup for 2 minutes, stirring constantly.

Ladle into soup bowls and garnish with the snipped fennel fronds.

White Bean and
Red Bell Pepper Soup with Garlic and Basil

SERVES 8

If they had beauty contests for soups, this one would win the crown hands down—and it wouldn't need to blush upon accepting the prize because it's a lovely shade of red to begin with. It's so pretty, as a matter of fact, that to say it's also robust is almost uncomplimentary. Blame it on the beans. They add solidity and texture and a lot of nutrition to boot. The soup is somewhat Italian in its inspiration and fresh flavor—based loosely on a pasta sauce we make often during the summer, when red bell peppers are gloriously plump and vivid—and the price is right!

In a soup kettle or large saucepan over moderate heat, bring the oil to rippling. Add the onion and garlic and cook, stirring, until softened, about 3 minutes. Stir in the peppers and cook for 8 minutes more or until the peppers are soft. Add the broth and the basil, increase the heat to high, and bring to a boil. Reduce the heat to simmer and cook, covered, for 15 minutes more.

Transfer the red pepper mixture in batches to a food processor and pulse several times to obtain a coarse mixture; do not puree. Return the mixture to the kettle over moderate heat, mix in the beans, salt, and pepper, and reheat for 2 minutes.

Serve in warm soup bowls garnished with chopped basil.

2 tablespoons olive oil

2 medium yellow onions, coarsely chopped

1 large garlic clove, coarsely chopped

4 red bell peppers, seeded, deveined, and cut into 1/2-inch pieces

1 quart chicken broth

1/2 cup firmly packed chopped fresh basil leaves, plus additional chopped leaves for garnishing if desired

1 15-ounce can white beans, drained, rinsed, and coarsely mashed with a fork

salt and freshly ground pepper to taste

Quick Pasta & Fagioli
(Italian White Bean and Pasta Soup)

Our traditional Venetian recipe for pasta e fagioli takes about 2 hours to cook. This one hits the soup bowls in less than a quarter of the time. Serve it as a soup (thinned, it will serve 6), as a pasta course, or as a one-dish meal with salad, bread, and fruit.

$^{1}/_{4}$ pound pancetta (Italian bacon) or prosciutto, chopped

2 tablespoons olive oil

1 medium onion, finely chopped

1 large carrot, finely chopped

1 large celery rib with leaves, finely chopped

3 large garlic cloves, finely chopped

3 tablespoons finely chopped fresh basil leaves

2 15-ounce cans white beans, drained and rinsed

1 15-ounce can imported Italian tomatoes, drained and chopped

2 teaspoons fresh rosemary leaves or 1 teaspoon dried, crushed

$^{1}/_{4}$ teaspoon hot red pepper flakes or more to taste

2 large fresh sage leaves or $^{1}/_{4}$ teaspoon dried

6 cups hot chicken broth or more for a thinner consistency (see note)

salt and freshly ground pepper to taste

2 cups dried fettuccine, tagliatelle, or egg noodles, broken into small pieces

$^{1}/_{2}$ cup minced fresh parsley leaves

$^{1}/_{2}$ cup freshly grated Parmesan cheese

In a large saucepan or soup kettle over moderate heat, cook the pancetta, stirring, until it is lightly browned, about 3 minutes. Pour off any fat and add the olive oil. When the oil is hot but not smoking, cook the onion, carrot, and celery until the onion is softened, about 5 minutes. Stir in the garlic and basil and cook for 1 minute more.

In a bowl, mash 1 cup of the beans and stir them into the pancetta mixture along with the remaining whole beans, tomatoes, rosemary, red pepper flakes, and sage. Pour the hot broth into the vegetables and simmer the mixture, covered, for about 5 minutes. Add salt and plenty of freshly ground pepper.

Stir in the pasta and cook for 8 to 10 minutes more or until the pasta is al dente. Stir in the parsley and serve the soup ladled into bowls and sprinkled with the Parmesan. Pass additional Parmesan at the table if desired.

Note: If the soup is thicker than you'd like it, thin it with a little additional hot broth or water. Remember, the pasta absorbs a good deal of liquid, so wait until the pasta has cooked before adding more broth.

We use dried fettuccine, tagliatelle, or other egg noodles broken into small pieces. But you can substitute any small tubular pasta such as tubetti or small shells or small bow ties. They're not traditional, but then again, neither is this recipe. The taste, however, is almost indistinguishable from the long-cooking original—if anything, this one is a bit fresher tasting.

Earthy White Bean Soup with Rosemary

We discovered long ago that root vegetables such as carrots and potatoes cook much faster cut into small pieces. This seems obvious, but it's something that even experienced cooks forget. If you're making mashed potatoes and want the potatoes to cook quickly, cut them into tiny dice and you can cut the boiling time by 10 to 15 minutes. In this soup we use carrots and parsnips to add sweetness and flavor to the beans but grate them to pare down the cooking time. After all, it's not their texture we're after; the soup is almost a puree, thick and luscious, perfumed with rosemary and just a touch of vinegar to contrast with the vegetables' sweetness.

2 tablespoons unsalted butter or olive oil

1 large garlic clove, minced

1 medium onion, finely chopped

1 small celery rib with leaves, finely chopped

1 carrot, grated

1 parsnip, grated

3 cups chicken broth

1 teaspoon minced fresh rosemary leaves or $1/2$ teaspoon dried, crushed

1 19-ounce can cannellini, chickpeas, or fava beans, drained, rinsed, and mashed well with a potato masher

1 teaspoon white wine vinegar

salt and freshly ground pepper to taste

$1/3$ cup minced fresh parsley leaves

In a large saucepan over moderate heat, bring the butter to foaming. When the foam subsides, cook the garlic, onion, celery, carrot, and parsnip, stirring, until the vegetables are tender, about 5 minutes. Stir in the broth and rosemary, increase the heat to moderately high, bring the mixture to a boil, and cook, stirring occasionally for 3 minutes.

Whisk in the beans a little at a time and return to a boil. Whisk in the vinegar, salt, and pepper. Add the parsley, cook for 2 minutes more, and serve piping hot.

Country White Bean, Sage, and Garlic Soup

SERVES 4

This soup takes only about 20 minutes from start to finish, but it has a strength of flavor and the heartiness of any soup cooked the laborious traditional way. You can make it even more robust by toasting four thin slices of French bread, setting them in the bottom of four soup bowls, and ladling the finished soup over them. A sprinkle of grated Gruyère or Parmesan can add still another flavor and a touch of elegance. At times we've also garnished the soup with chopped walnuts or hazelnuts instead of the cheese—an unexpected but welcome flavor and texture innovation.

In a medium saucepan over moderate heat, bring the oil to rippling and stir in the sage, garlic, and bay leaf, crushing them with a wooden spoon and cooking the mixture until it is fragrant, about 2 minutes.

Increase the heat to moderately high and add the broth, beans, salt, and pepper. Bring to a boil, reduce the heat to simmer, and cook, partially covered, for 15 minutes.

With a slotted spoon, find and discard the bay leaf. Remove the pan from the heat and whisk the egg into the soup.

Arrange the toasts in the bottom of 4 soup bowls and ladle the soup over them. Sprinkle each serving with 1 tablespoon of the grated Gruyère. Serve immediately.

1 tablespoon olive oil

2 tablespoons minced fresh sage leaves

4 large garlic cloves, minced

1 bay leaf

1 quart chicken broth

1 15-ounce can white beans, drained, rinsed, and lightly crushed

1/2 teaspoon salt or to taste

1/2 teaspoon freshly ground pepper or to taste

1 large egg, beaten lightly

4 thin slices French bread, toasted

1/4 cup grated Gruyère cheese or 4 teaspoons grated Parmesan cheese

Moldavian-Style White Bean and Sausage Soup

Most thick and hearty peasant soups get that way from hours of cooking. Not this one. It's done in just 25 minutes, including preparation time. We like to serve it along with a good loaf of black bread and a salad and call it dinner. There's even enough for a second helping for those who don't think just soup is a meal. You can double the amount of franks if you want even more to chew on or change the franks to cubed ham or small chunks of meat loaf, if you want to use up some leftovers.

3 cups canned cannellini, drained, rinsed, and crushed

3 cups chicken broth

2 medium boiling potatoes, peeled and cut into $^1/_2$-inch dice

2 tablespoons olive or canola oil or unsalted butter

1 large onion, finely chopped

3 large garlic cloves, thinly sliced

1 leek, white part only, washed thoroughly and finely chopped

2 kosher-style frankfurters or $^1/_4$ pound kielbasa, cut into $^1/_2$-inch pieces

1 teaspoon fresh thyme leaves or $^1/_2$ teaspoon dried, crumbled

$^1/_2$ teaspoon salt or to taste

$^1/_2$ teaspoon freshly ground white pepper or to taste

1 tablespoon red wine vinegar or more to taste

paprika for garnish

In a soup kettle or large sauté pan over medium-high heat, stir the beans and broth together and bring to a boil. Add the potatoes, lower the heat to simmer, and cook, partially covered, until the potatoes are almost tender, about 8 minutes.

Meanwhile, heat the oil to rippling in a small skillet over medium heat. Add the onion, garlic, and leek and cook, stirring occasionally, until the vegetables are soft but not colored, about 5 minutes. Add the frankfurters and cook for 2 minutes more.

Stir the vegetable-frankfurter mixture into the bean and potato soup, add the thyme, salt, and pepper, stir well, and simmer, covered, until the potatoes are tender, about 5 to 10 minutes.

Remove the soup from the heat and add the vinegar. Let stand for a few minutes, taste for seasoning, and add more vinegar, salt, and pepper if necessary. Ladle into warm soup bowls and garnish each serving with a dash of paprika.

ACCOMPANYING
DISHES

Chickpeas with Fried Bread Crumbs, Garlic, and Sesame Paste

SERVES 4

For the bread crumbs in this dish we like to use fresh sourdough bread or rolls crumbed in the blender or food processor and then fried in good light olive oil or butter. This substantial side dish tastes like chewy hummus and can be served hot or at room temperature. It works equally well with lamb chops, a roast, or grilled fish. It's also good over small pasta shapes like shells or farfalle. Allow about $^1/_4$ pound of pasta per person (the recipe will then serve 6) and toss well before serving.

In a large skillet or sauté pan, bring the oil to rippling. Over moderately high heat, stir in the bread crumbs and lower the heat to moderate. Cook, stirring constantly, until the bread crumbs begin to brown. Add the garlic and sauté for about 1 minute more.

Turn the heat to moderately low and stir in the sesame paste (tahini) and lemon juice until they are well combined with the bread crumbs. Stir in the chickpeas and continue to cook for 2 minutes more or until the chickpeas are heated through. Taste and add salt and pepper if desired. Fold in the minced parsley and serve hot or let cool to room temperature.

$^1/_4$ cup light olive oil

$1^1/_4$ cups fine fresh bread crumbs (preferably sourdough)

6 garlic cloves, finely chopped

$^1/_2$ cup sesame paste (tahini)

juice of 1 lemon

1 19-ounce can chickpeas, drained and rinsed

salt and freshly ground pepper if desired

$^1/_4$ cup packed minced fresh parsley

Mashed Black-Eyed Peas Spiked with Horseradish

SERVES 4

Mashed black-eyed peas may never replace mashed potatoes as an American tradition, but they really are good, especially with horseradish to give them a kick. Taste these, and you'll agree that they deserve a place on the dinner plate heaped next to thin slices of smoked ham, savory meat loaf, or roast loin of pork.

1 cup water

2 15-ounce cans black-eyed
    peas, drained and rinsed

2 tablespoons unsalted butter,
    softened

2 tablespoons bottled
    horseradish

salt and freshly ground
    pepper to taste

In a saucepan over moderately high heat, bring the water to a boil, add the black-eyed peas, and cook, uncovered, until just heated through, about 2 minutes. Drain the peas, return them to the saucepan, turn the heat to low, and fold in the butter and horseradish.

Mash the mixture with a potato masher or large fork, season with salt and pepper, transfer to a serving bowl, and bring to the table steaming.

Plain Ol' Black-Eyed Peas in Tomato Sauce with Cilantro

SERVES 8

Black-eyed peas turn up as New Year's food in the American South and in many parts of Africa, but there's no need to wait for December 31 to enjoy them. Save this savory, fragrant dish for New Year's if you like, but your family and friends won't want to wait 12 months to have it again. They're supposed to bring a year of good luck.

In a saucepan over moderate heat, bring the oil to rippling. Add the garlic and cook, stirring, until golden, about 1 minute. Add half the cilantro and everything else but the rice. Simmer the mixture, covered, for about 10 minutes.

On a round serving platter, arrange the rice around the edge with a well in the center, fill the well with the black-eyed pea mixture, and sprinkle the remaining cilantro over the top.

3 tablespoons olive oil

1 heaped tablespoon minced garlic

2 tablespoons minced cilantro leaves

1 8-ounce can tomato sauce or 1 cup homemade

2 15-ounce cans black-eyed peas, drained and rinsed

$1/2$ teaspoon salt or to taste

$1/2$ teaspoon freshly ground pepper or more to taste

4 cups cooked rice for serving

Cannellini with Basil, Sorrel, Scallions, and Sour Cream

Sorrel (sour grass), scallions, and sour cream have a natural affinity. We've discovered that beans and basil fit right in with this lively threesome. The sorrel gives the dish a wonderfully elegant tartness. It should be wilted, not cooked.

1 tablespoon olive oil

1 tablespoon canola or vegetable oil

2 15-ounce cans small cannellini, drained and rinsed

¼ cup shredded fresh basil leaves

¼ cup shredded fresh sorrel leaves

1 scallion, both white and green parts, thinly sliced

2 tablespoons sour cream

½ teaspoon salt

½ teaspoon freshly ground pepper

In a large skillet or sauté pan over moderately high heat, bring the oils to rippling. Add the cannellini and sauté, stirring, for 2 or 3 minutes or until heated through and browned slightly. Add the basil, sorrel, and scallion to the beans and toss the mixture briefly. Remove the skillet from the heat and mix in the sour cream, salt, and pepper. Blend well and serve.

Cannellini with Arugula and Garlic

SERVES 4

Friends in Italy served this combination to us, and at the time it seemed inspired. Now it seems to us almost inevitable. The robustness of the beans and garlic, the strong taste of arugula, and the warm bite of red pepper form a dish sturdy enough to hold its own with almost any main dish. It's certainly assertive enough to serve as a starter, stimulating the tastebuds, heralding more appetite pleasers to come.

In a large sauté pan or skillet over moderately low heat, bring the oil to rippling. Add the garlic and red pepper flakes and cook, stirring, for 2 minutes. Add the arugula, still stirring, and cook it until it begins to wilt, a minute or two more.

Increase the heat to moderate, add the broth, and simmer, stirring, for 3 minutes. Add the beans and salt and continue to cook, stirring gently, for 2 minutes more or until the beans are heated through.

Transfer the bean mixture to a serving bowl, sprinkle it with Parmesan, and serve.

2 tablespoons olive oil

4 large garlic cloves, thinly sliced

$1/2$ teaspoon hot red pepper flakes or more to taste

3 bunches of arugula (about 1 pound), coarsely chopped

$1/2$ cup chicken broth

1 19-ounce can cannellini, drained and rinsed

$1/2$ teaspoon salt or to taste

freshly grated Parmesan or Romano cheese for serving

Cannellini and Parsnips with Lemon Zest

SERVES 8

Parsnips are sweet and spicy tasting, and they cook in just 10 minutes if you shred them first. In this recipe they're paired felicitously with cannellini for body and made more piquant with a touch of lemon zest. This is the kind of surprisingly simple, elegant side dish that, although it takes almost no time to prepare, garners lots of kudos from family or guests.

$^2/_3$ cup water or canned
    chicken broth

$^1/_4$ cup unsalted butter

1 teaspoon salt or to taste

$^1/_2$ teaspoon freshly ground
    white pepper

2 pounds parsnips, peeled
    and coarsely shredded

1 15-ounce can cannellini,
    drained and rinsed

1 teaspoon finely grated
    lemon zest

1 tablespoon chopped fresh
    parsley leaves for garnish

In a large saucepan over moderately high heat, bring the water, butter, salt, and pepper to a boil. Add the parsnips, cover, and reduce the heat to simmer. Cook, stirring occasionally, for 10 minutes, until tender and almost all the liquid has been absorbed. Add the beans and lemon zest, stir well, and cook for 2 minutes more or until the beans are heated through.

Transfer to a warm serving dish and sprinkle with the parsley.

Golden Bean Pancakes with Olives and Capers

SERVES 4

You can make these pancakes with beans pureed from scratch or with leftover bean puree you happen to have on hand. Either way the result will be crisp on the outside, golden and savory on the inside. The pancakes have character, a bold, full flavor—so they're a sturdy companion for a meat or poultry main dish. Try serving them with wedges of lemon for diners to add a sunny, sharp note.

In a food processor, puree the beans with the garlic and turmeric. Transfer to a bowl and stir in the capers, olives, pepper, salt, and egg.

Scoop up 1/4 cup at a time and form into 1/2-inch-thick cakes. Coat the cakes well with the bread crumbs, pressing them lightly into the surface. The pancakes can be made 1 day in advance, covered with plastic wrap, and chilled.

In a sauté pan or large skillet over moderately high heat, bring the oil to rippling. Add the pancakes and sauté, turning them once, for 4 minutes or until they are nicely browned.

Serve the pancakes with lemon wedges or sprinkled with the cilantro leaves if you like.

Note: It's easy to vary the flavoring of these pancakes. Instead of the capers and olives, blend in a tablespoon or more of bottled Asian black bean and garlic sauce; or mix in some curry powder or garam masala, minced hot green pepper, and chopped scallions; or add finely chopped onion and minced leftover vegetables.

They can also become the underpinnings for another dish, especially one with a sauce that can be spooned over the pancakes, such as a fish stew or a mélange of beans and young vegetables.

They're lovely, too, served as part of a breakfast or brunch plate.

1 15-ounce can cannellini, drained and rinsed

1 large garlic clove, chopped

1/2 teaspoon ground turmeric

1 tablespoon drained bottled capers, finely chopped

8 Kalamata or other brine-cured black olives, pitted and finely chopped

1/2 teaspoon freshly ground pepper or more to taste

salt to taste

1 large egg, beaten lightly

1/2 cup dry bread crumbs

1/4 cup canola or vegetable oil

lemon wedges or minced cilantro leaves if desired

Fava Beans with Tomatoes and Portobello Mushrooms

SERVES 4 TO 6

Fava beans were the only beans known to Europeans before the discovery of the New World introduced the kidney bean in all its various guises and disguises. Favas are hardly ever seen on American tables unless the family is Italian, Greek, Spanish, or Egyptian. This is unfortunate; the fava has a wonderfully earthy flavor different from the nuttiness of most beans. Don't confuse it with the lima bean, which it resembles in shape but not in color or taste. Because the dried beans require long soaking, sometimes a day and a half, and at least an hour of cooking before becoming tender, we recommend using the canned variety (or fresh, if you can find them, in early spring). This recipe combines them (cooked just long enough to heat through, to retain their special quality) with mushrooms, another earthy flavor, and the vibrant tang of tomatoes.

2 tablespoons olive oil

2 tablespoons finely chopped garlic

$1/2$ pound portobello mushrooms, cut into $1/4$-inch strips

1 28-ounce can Italian plum tomatoes with their juice

1 teaspoon Italian seasoning

$1/2$ teaspoon dried oregano

1 teaspoon freshly ground pepper

2 tablespoons chopped fresh parsley

2 15-ounce cans fava beans, drained and rinsed

In a large skillet or sauté pan over moderately high heat, bring the oil to rippling. Add the garlic and sauté until it just begins to turn golden, about 1 minute. Raise the heat to high and stir in the mushrooms, continuing to stir until they wilt and begin to turn brown, 3 to 5 minutes.

Add the tomatoes, cutting them coarsely as you drop them into the pan (or break them up with your fingers), tomato juice, Italian seasoning, oregano, pepper, and parsley. Bring just to a boil, then lower the heat to simmer and cook for 5 minutes, stirring occasionally. Stir in the fava beans and cook for 2 minutes more or until the beans are just heated through. Serve immediately.

Green Beans with Kalamata Olives and Cashews

We like green beans plain but often fancy them up, as we do here, in Middle Eastern style with olives and cashews. These two extra, but not irrelevant, ingredients are almost ornamental, like jewelry on a well-cut basic black dress—adding sparkle and a unique flavor contrast to the oil-slicked, crisp-cooked beans.

In a large sauté pan or skillet over moderately high heat, cook the beans in the water, covered, for 3 minutes or until they are crisp-tender.

Add the oil, stir to coat the beans well, and continue to cook, uncovered, stirring occasionally, until most of the liquid has evaporated, about 3 minutes more.

Add the olives and half the cashews and cook the mixture, stirring, for 2 to 3 minutes or until all the liquid has evaporated.

Season with salt and pepper and serve garnished with the remaining cashews.

1 pound green beans, trimmed and cut into 1-inch pieces

$^1/_4$ cup water

2 tablespoons light olive oil

$^1/_2$ cup pitted Kalamata olives, thinly sliced

$^1/_2$ cup roasted cashews, finely chopped

salt and freshly ground pepper to taste

Green Beans with Hazelnuts, Mustard Seeds, and Cilantro

Green beans can be prepared in many ways, but as a side dish we like to keep them simple, just steamed, with a dressing that often includes nuts. Lately we've become very partial to hazelnuts. Many cooks avoid hazelnuts because they think they must skin them before using them in a recipe. This is true only when the thin, papery skin would be unsightly as in some baked goods, in an elegantly presented dish, or when their brown color is not wanted. In this dish you can remove the skins or not. Along with mustard seeds and cilantro leaves, the hazelnuts bring out the green beans' elusive garden-fresh flavor. Just be sure the beans are not overcooked—tender but crisp.

1 pound young green beans, cut into 2-inch lengths

2 tablespoons unsalted butter

1 teaspoon black mustard seeds (available at Indian markets and some specialty food stores)

$1/2$ cup chopped hazelnuts

$1/2$ teaspoon salt or to taste

$1/2$ teaspoon freshly ground pepper

2 tablespoons finely chopped cilantro leaves

In a steamer filled with boiling water to just below the steamer basket, steam the beans over moderately high heat for 5 to 6 minutes or until barely tender and still-very crisp. Refresh the beans under cold running water and drain well. Set aside.

While the beans are steaming, in a large skillet or sauté pan over moderately high heat, bring the butter to foaming. When the foam subsides and the butter is just beginning to color, add the mustard seeds and hazelnuts and cook, stirring often, until the hazelnuts are browned lightly, about 5 minutes.

Stir in the partially cooked green beans, salt, pepper, and cilantro, reduce the heat to moderately low, and cook the mixture, covered, stirring occasionally, for about 3 minutes or until the beans are just crisp-tender.

Green Beans with Small Red Potatoes, Red Onion, and Olives

SERVES 4

The fresher the green beans, the more quickly they cook. We even like them raw, so they taste best to us a little crisp. Of course they're lovely alone, with just a touch of butter or olive oil and some salt and pepper to bring out their fresh flavor. But often we combine them with other vegetables whose textures and flavors contrast with the crunchy beans. This time it's potatoes, with a vinegar and oil dressing punctuated with the sharp saltiness of Kalamata or other brine-cured olives and the sweet sting of onions. We steam the potatoes along with the beans. The two vegetables take about the same time to cook if the potatoes are new and small enough to be cut into tiny quarters (if not, cut the potatoes into $1/2$-inch dice). They need not be peeled.

In a serving bowl, stir together the onion, vinegar, salt, pepper, and olive oil. Let the mixture stand while you cook the green beans and potatoes.

In a steamer set over boiling water, steam the beans and potatoes together for 8 minutes or until they are just tender. Add them to the dressing while they are still hot and toss them well with the olives. Serve warm or at room temperature.

1 cup chopped red onion

1 tablespoon red wine vinegar

$1/2$ teaspoon salt or to taste

$1/2$ teaspoon freshly ground pepper or more to taste

1 tablespoon olive oil

$1/2$ pound green beans, cut into thirds

1 pound tiny red Bliss potatoes, quartered

10 Kalamata or other brine-cured black olives, pitted and thinly sliced

Lima Bean, Potato, and Garlic Puree with Crushed Potato Chips

SERVES 6

We must confess: of all the beans, lima beans are our least favorite. Maybe it's because they were the bean of choice in Depression kitchens and our mothers served them boiled, with no butter, no seasoning, nothing to bring them to life on the plate. They just lay there waiting for someone to say, "If you don't eat your lima beans, you don't get any dessert!" Who wouldn't resent them? Old prejudices die hard, but since then we've learned to . . . well . . . like them, especially hidden in a stew or pureed with other ingredients as we've done here. Then the texture changes and their slightly nutty flavor is all that remains to add character to the potato and garlic combination. The crushed potato chips are an unexpected and welcome contribution—adding crunch as well as eye appeal to the dish. Incidentally, the garlic loses its bite when boiled.

1 pound russet (baking) potatoes or yellow-fleshed potatoes, peeled and cut into 1-inch pieces

6 large garlic cloves

2 10-ounce packages frozen baby lima beans

1/2 cup regular, low-fat, or nonfat plain yogurt or 3 tablespoons unsalted butter

salt and freshly ground white pepper to taste

1 cup crushed potato chips

In a large saucepan over moderate heat, combine the potatoes and garlic with enough water to cover by 1 inch. Simmer, covered, for about 8 minutes. Add the lima beans and simmer, covered, for 8 minutes more or until the potatoes are tender.

Drain the vegetables, saving some of the cooking liquid, and puree them in a food processor, adding enough reserved cooking liquid to produce a nice consistency, until they are smooth.

Transfer to a serving bowl and stir in the yogurt, salt, and pepper. Sprinkle the top with the crushed potato chips and serve.

Creamy Minted Pea Puree

For an elaborate holiday dinner, we like the vegetable accompaniments to be simple and quick to prepare—but we also like them to be impressive and hold their own with the rest of the dishes. This pea puree is so delicious no one ever believes that it's ready to serve in less than 10 minutes. Serve it with a crown roast, leg of lamb, roast turkey, a fresh ham, or other holiday fare and feast away!

In a large saucepan over moderately high heat, boil the peas and mint leaves in the water, covered, for 3 minutes. Drain the mixture and puree it in a food processor with the remaining ingredients, stopping to scrape down the sides, until the mixture is smooth.

Transfer the puree to a serving dish and garnish with the mint sprigs. Serve immediately.

2 10-ounce packages frozen tiny peas (petits pois), thawed

$1/4$ cup fresh mint leaves plus mint sprigs for garnish

$1/2$ cup water

2 tablespoons half-and-half

2 tablespoons unsalted butter, cut into small pieces

salt and freshly ground pepper to taste

Tiny Peas Braised with Scallions and Mint

SERVES 4

What could be better with lamb chops than garlic-mashed potatoes and a bright green mound of peas? Here we braise them with scallions and flavor them with a little fresh mint. Remember when lamb was always served with a dollop of kelly-green mint jelly on the plate? It's a memory we choose to forget. But just a hint of mint with peas is a lovely combination, and it's a nice fresh flavor to counter the gaminess of lamb. Consequently, these peas are a good foil for lamb kabobs, lamb stew, or butterflied leg of lamb—or with any grilled, broiled, or panfried meat or fish.

1 tablespoon unsalted butter

1/2 teaspoon sugar

6 scallions, both white and green parts, cut into 1-inch pieces

1/2 teaspoon salt or to taste

1/2 teaspoon freshly ground pepper or to taste

1/3 cup chicken broth

1 10-ounce package frozen tiny peas (petits pois)

2 tablespoons minced fresh mint leaves

In a saucepan over moderate heat, melt the butter. When the foam subsides, add the sugar, scallions, salt, and pepper and cook, stirring, for 2 minutes. Add the broth and simmer the mixture, partially covered, for 2 minutes more.

Increase the heat to high, add the peas, and cook, uncovered, for 2 minutes or until most of the liquid has evaporated. Stir in the mint and serve.

Petits Pois with Sweet Butter and Lemon Zest

SERVES 6

Peas are one of the few vegetables we find are almost better frozen than they are fresh. Who knows how long "fresh" pea pods have been languishing in the greengrocer's bins, while frozen peas are put into a lovely state of suspended animation only hours after they are picked. Tiny young peas are best. They are usually in the frozen food case labeled "tiny peas" or "petits pois" and come in 10-ounce packages or 20-ounce bags. The little peas in the bags are more economical and great to have in the freezer to add at the last minute to rice, soups, and stews. They're frozen in a lump but are easily separated by tapping the bag sharply on a work surface. Once separated, they can be weighed and measured just like fresh peas. Just take the quantity you need and return the rest to the freezer. Try this simple recipe with frozen black-eyed peas, too.

In a large skillet over moderate heat, bring the butter to foaming. When the foam subsides, add the peas and cook, stirring, until heated through, about 2 minutes. Stir in salt and pepper to taste, transfer to a serving bowl, and sprinkle with the zest.

Note: This recipe can be made with completely frozen peas, in which case the cooking time should be increased by 1 minute.

2 tablespoons unsalted butter

2 10-ounce packages frozen tiny peas (petits pois) or 1 20-ounce package, barely thawed

salt and freshly ground pepper to taste

the zest of 1 lemon (use a vegetable peeler), cut into fine julienne strips

Warm Pink Beans, Beets, and Walnuts

Serve this side dish, first course, or salad warm, cold, or at room temperature. It combines several tastes and textures from sweet to sharp and soft to crunchy. The color is beautiful, a rich magenta dotted with the green and white of the scallions and cilantro. Altogether it's a festive dish that works best with simple main courses like grilled meat, fish, or chicken. We also like it the way it was served to us in Paris, with Matjes herring fillets accompanied by black bread with butter. The only change we've made is to substitute beans for the peeled, diced grapefruit sections the French seem to love to add to some salads—why, we don't know. We love grapefruit, too, but it never seems to harmonize with other flavors and offers a singularly harsh note here.

1 16-ounce can sliced beets, drained, liquid reserved, and beet slices cut in half

4 large garlic cloves

1 15-ounce can pink beans, drained and rinsed

2 tablespoons olive oil

2 tablespoons minced cilantro leaves

3 tablespoons red wine vinegar or to taste

2 scallions, both white and green parts, very thinly sliced

salt and freshly ground pepper to taste

12 walnut halves, toasted and chopped

In a small saucepan over moderately high heat, bring the reserved liquid from the canned beets to a boil and in it cook the garlic cloves for 5 minutes or until they are softened. With a slotted spoon, transfer the garlic to a cutting board.

Add the beets and beans to the liquid remaining in the pan, reduce the heat to moderate, and cook for 2 minutes or until the beets and beans are heated through. Drain the mixture and transfer the vegetables to a serving bowl.

Mash the reserved garlic to a paste with the flat side of a heavy knife and in a small bowl stir it together with the oil, cilantro, vinegar, scallions, salt, and pepper. Toss the beet/bean mixture with the dressing, adjust the seasoning if necessary, and sprinkle with the chopped walnuts. Serve warm, cold, or at room temperature.

Snow Peas and Green Beans with Toasted Sesame Seeds

This is a room-temperature side dish—almost a salad—that blends nicely with grilled meats, poultry, or fish. It's especially good with chicken or fish teriyaki. Both the snow peas and the green beans are quickly stir-fried to retain freshness and crunch, then tossed with a lightly vinegared dressing and toasted sesame seeds. Because vegetables like these can be eaten raw, they are in the pan only until they are crisp-tender—under 5 minutes. When in season, sugar snap peas can be substituted for snow peas.

In a small bowl, whisk together the vinegar, oil, Maggi, salt, and pepper.

In a large saucepan of boiling salted water cook the green beans for 4 minutes, add the snow peas, and cook for 30 seconds more.

Drain the vegetables and transfer them immediately to a bowl of ice and cold water to stop the cooking. When cool, drain and pat the vegetables dry with paper towels and in a bowl toss them with the sesame seeds and the dressing.

1 tablespoon rice or white wine vinegar

2 tablespoons Asian toasted sesame oil

4 dashes of Maggi seasoning

salt and freshly ground pepper to taste

1/2 pound green beans, cut diagonally into 1-inch pieces

1/2 pound snow peas, strings discarded, cut diagonally into thirds

2 tablespoons sesame seeds, lightly toasted

Plain and Simple Buttered
Snow Peas or Sugar Snap Peas

SERVES 4

Snow peas cook crisp-tender in just 1 minute. So do sugar snap peas. Both are deli-cious raw, so the brief cooking just heats them up. The butter is mere gloss, an embell-ishment that could be heightened with a teaspoon of minced garlic or shallot tossed in before serving or a tablespoon or two of black bean sauce (page 234). How you season them depends on what you are serving them with, the texture and seasoning of the plate's main event. You might also try them blanched and chilled as a salad burnished with a lemony vinaigrette or cut into thirds and add raw to a green salad.

¹/₂ **pound snow peas or sugar snap peas or a combination, trimmed and strings discarded**

1 **tablespoon unsalted butter, softened**

In a large saucepan over high heat, bring salt-ed water to a boil and in it blanch the snow peas or sugar snap peas for 1 minute or until just crisp-tender. Drain them well and toss them with the butter to coat.

Mashed Red Bean and Whipped Cream Gratin

We don't often use heavy cream in a recipe, but when we do you can be sure it's worth the extra calories and cholesterol. The color combination alone is a surprise, pink and white. But it's the flavor and texture of this dish that make it extraordinary. The recipe is based on a mashed potato dish we had at the spectacular Boston restaurant Biba. Please use Parmigiano-Reggiano or Grana (Italian Parmesan-style cheese made outside the region of Parma) in the topping, not "imported Parmesan," which is usually from Argentina and nothing like the real stuff.

Preheat the oven to 500°.

In a bowl with an electric mixer, whip the cream until it holds soft peaks and fold in the Gruyère. Set aside.

In a saucepan over moderately low heat, bring the butter to foaming. When the foam subsides, cook the garlic in it until it begins to turn golden, about 1 minute. Stir in the salt, pepper, and pureed beans.

Cook the bean mixture, stirring, for 2 minutes or until it is heated through. Add the milk and stir until smooth and combined well.

Spread the bean mixture in a shallow 12-inch oval gratin dish. Spread the reserved cream mixture over the beans and sprinkle with the Parmesan. Bake the gratin in the center of the oven until heated through and the topping is golden brown, about 10 minutes. Serve immediately.

$^3/_4$ cup heavy cream

1 cup grated Gruyère cheese (about 4 ounces)

$^1/_2$ stick ($^1/_4$ cup) unsalted butter

2 large garlic cloves, minced

1 teaspoon salt or to taste

$^1/_2$ teaspoon freshly ground white pepper

3 15-ounce cans red beans, drained, rinsed, and pureed

$^3/_4$ cup warm milk

3 tablespoons freshly grated Parmesan cheese

Spicy Red Lentils and Tomatoes

SERVES 4

What was once a soup we have recast as a side dish. Barely moist instead of liquid, it's perfect with roasted or grilled meat, fish, or poultry. The flavor is forceful and zingy, the color sort of rich pinkish yellow. Red lentils cook quickly and hardly hold their shape.

1 cup red lentils

2 tablespoons canola oil

2 medium onions, coarsely
 chopped

6 large garlic cloves, coarsely
 chopped

2 tablespoons grated fresh
 ginger

1 teaspoon ground cumin

1 teaspoon ground coriander

$1/4$ teaspoon hot red pepper
 flakes

$1/2$ teaspoon ground turmeric

salt and freshly ground
 pepper to taste

2 cups chicken broth

1 cup drained canned
 tomatoes

cilantro leaves for garnish if
 desired

In a large bowl, pick over and wash the lentils in a few changes of cold water, and when the water is clear, drain them in a fine sieve and set aside.

In a large saucepan over moderate heat, bring the oil to rippling. Add the onions and cook, stirring, until they are softened, about 5 minutes. Add the garlic and ginger and cook, stirring, for 1 minute more. Add the cumin, coriander, red pepper flakes, turmeric, salt, and pepper, reduce the heat to moderately low, and cook, stirring, for 1 minute. Add the lentils, broth, and tomatoes and simmer, covered, for 15 to 20 minutes or until the lentils are tender, adding a little more broth or water if the mixture becomes too dry.

In a blender or food processor, puree the mixture in batches, transferring it to a serving bowl as it is pureed. Garnish with cilantro leaves if desired.

Note: To make this into a delicious bread spread, drain the solids in a sieve, then puree them in a blender or food processor, adding a little more oil.

Mashed White Beans
and Root Vegetables with Horseradish

SERVES 4

Beans and root vegetables have been kept apart long enough. Here we bring them together—three roots and a bean, embracing in a richly flavored, luxuriously textured comfort food that offers a new and stylish approach to homey peasant fare. This is the kind of food that it's hard to keep scavengers away from—the cook being the most tempted of all. Frankly, we've been known to serve scanty portions of this dish just because we couldn't keep the tasting spoon out of the pot up until serving time.

In a large saucepan of boiling salted water, cook the turnips, parsnips, and potatoes for 10 to 12 minutes or until tender.

Meanwhile, in a small saucepan over low heat, stir together the bean puree, milk, butter, and horseradish until the mixture is hot and keep it warm.

Drain the vegetables and, over high heat, shake the pan for 30 seconds or until all the excess liquid is evaporated. Reduce the heat to low and add the bean mixture to the vegetables, mash them together with a potato masher until they are smooth, and stir in salt and pepper to taste. Serve immediately.

2 white turnips, peeled and cut into $1/2$-inch pieces

3 parsnips, peeled and cut into $1/2$-inch pieces

2 russet potatoes, peeled and cut into $1/2$-inch pieces *just before cooking* or peeled and cut and covered with cold water

1 10-ounce can cannellini, drained, rinsed, and pureed

$1/4$ cup milk

$1/2$ stick ($1/4$ cup) unsalted butter

3 tablespoons drained bottled horseradish

salt and freshly ground pepper to taste

Puree of White Beans and Artichoke Hearts

SERVES 4

Pureed vegetables make an elegant side dish. They seem difficult to noncooks but are really very easy. All you need is a food mill or a food processor. In this recipe we like to use a food mill because the artichoke hearts have some fibrous leaves attached and we want this puree to be absolutely smooth. The food mill presses only the cooked, softened vegetables through the sieve, leaving the solids behind. This is done very quickly with only a few turns of the handle, so the puree stays hot. In a food processor pureeing to a comparable smoothness takes much longer and the puree would need to be reheated before serving. This puree tastes like the pure essence of artichoke mellowed with the beans and enlivened with the fresh bite of scallions.

1½ tablespoons unsalted butter

2 9-ounce packages frozen artichoke hearts, thawed and chopped

1 large garlic clove, minced

1 15-ounce can white beans, drained and rinsed

4 scallions, both white and green parts, very thinly sliced

salt and freshly ground white pepper to taste

In a large skillet or saucepan over moderate heat, melt the butter. When the foam subsides, cook the chopped artichoke hearts and garlic, stirring often, until the artichokes are very tender, about 5 minutes. Add the beans and cook, stirring, for 4 minutes more or until the beans are very hot and falling apart.

Force the artichoke/bean mixture through a food mill fitted with the medium disk into a heated serving bowl, discarding the solids. Fold in the scallions and season with salt and pepper. Serve immediately.

Note: This side dish can be turned into a lovely soup by adding 2 or 3 cups hot chicken broth to the puree, then stirring in the scallions. Garnish each soup bowl with a tiny sprig of fresh oregano, thyme, marjoram, parsley, or rosemary.

White Beans with Smoked Salmon and Dill Dressing

SERVES 4 TO 6

Here's a substantial side dish that can double as a salad course or first course, depending on your menu. For brunch its smoky flavor pairs nicely with scrambled eggs or crab cakes. Because it's served at room temperature, it can go along on a picnic. The recipe makes about 2 cups of dressing, which will keep, covered and chilled, for about a week. All alone with its combination of salmon, sour cream, and dill, it works wonders on salad greens or as a dip for chips or raw vegetables. Be sure to use a good-quality smoked salmon for this dish—either freshly sliced at the deli counter or in shrink wrap from the cold case—not the canned variety, which is often oily and salty.

In a food processor, blend the sour cream, mayonnaise, salmon, salt, pepper, vinegar, tomatoes, dill, and onion until the mixture is smooth.

In a serving bowl, fold the dressing gently into the beans until coated well. Sprinkle with more snipped dill and the capers, if you like, before serving.

$1/2$ cup sour cream

1 cup homemade or good-quality bottled mayonnaise

3 ounces smoked salmon

$1/2$ teaspoon salt or to taste

$1/2$ teaspoon freshly ground pepper

1 tablespoon white wine vinegar

$1/2$ cup chopped drained canned tomatoes

1 tablespoon snipped fresh dill, plus more for garnish if desired

1 medium red onion, coarsely chopped

2 15-ounce cans large white beans, drained and rinsed

1 tablespoon drained bottled capers for garnish if desired

White Beans with Fresh Tomatoes and Fresh Sage

Nothing can take the place of fresh ripe tomatoes, except, in certain recipes, imported canned Italian plum tomatoes. Like canned beans, canned Italian tomatoes are as close to the real thing as you can get—except for the texture. For cooking they're fine, as in this recipe. But please, use only fresh ripe tomatoes during the season.

2 tablespoons olive oil

12 fresh sage leaves or to taste

2 large garlic cloves, minced

2 large vine-ripened tomatoes, peeled, seeded, and diced, or 2 cups canned Italian plum tomatoes, drained and juice reserved

2 15-ounce cans cannellini, drained and rinsed

salt and freshly ground pepper to taste

In a large skillet or sauté pan over moderate heat, bring the oil to rippling and in it sauté the sage and garlic, stirring, until the sage begins to brown slightly, about 2 or 3 minutes. Stir in the tomatoes and cook for 2 minutes more, stirring, until a sauce begins to form.

Stir in the beans, salt, and add a generous amount of pepper, taste, reduce the heat to moderately low, and simmer for about 10 minutes, adding a little water (or some of the reserved tomato juice if using canned tomatoes) if necessary to keep the beans moist. Serve hot.

Note: Try using 2 teaspoons fresh rosemary leaves or 1/2 cup firmly packed basil instead of the sage.

White Bean and Watercress Gratin

SERVES 6 TO 8

This delicious side dish can also be served as an elegant first course. But we like it best as part of a Sunday supper to accompany roast beef or roast chicken. It takes only a few minutes to put together and spends most of its time—about 20 minutes—bubbling away in the oven while you busy yourself with more important things like conversation with your guests or making a salad. You can vary this recipe with sorrel leaves, replacing the watercress, when they are in season. The acerbic flavor of the greens lends a nice savor to the dish. Or try adding coarsely shredded radicchio for still another personality. One way to use this gratin is to arrange it on the plate as a bed on which to perch a grilled chicken breast, lamb chops, or a seared tuna steak.

Preheat the oven to 425°.

In a blender or food processor, puree 1 cup of the beans with the broth, oil, vinegar, salt, and pepper. Stir the mixture into the remaining whole beans and the watercress and spread into a 10-inch oval gratin dish.

In a bowl, combine the bread crumbs, Gruyère, and garlic and sprinkle the topping over the bean-watercress mixture. Bake the gratin in the middle of the oven for 20 minutes or until it is bubbly and golden. Serve at the table from the gratin dish or divide the gratin among 6 to 8 plates.

2 15-ounce cans white beans, drained and rinsed

1¹/₂ cups chicken broth

3 tablespoons olive oil

2 teaspoons white wine vinegar

1 teaspoon salt or to taste

¹/₂ teaspoon freshly ground pepper

1¹/₂ cups firmly packed watercress sprigs, coarsely chopped

1 cup fresh bread crumbs

1 cup grated Gruyère cheese

1 tablespoon minced garlic

ONE-DISH
MEALS

_____

Clams with Chinese Black Bean Sauce

In New York's Chinatown there's a restaurant that makes the best clams with black beans we have ever tasted. We've asked the kitchen to use the same fascinating sauce over shrimp, squid, or scallops, but the cook refuses. We've never figured out why. So, in desperation, we devised our own recipe, which we think rivals the original. Now we often substitute shrimp, squid, or scallops quickly stir-fried (for only 1 or 2 minutes) for the steamed clams in this recipe, and, of course, it works just fine. You can get the Asian ingredients at Asian food markets, specialty food stores, and some supermarkets.

1 tablespoon cornstarch

³/₄ cup cold water

2¹/₂ tablespoons oyster sauce

1 teaspoon dark soy sauce

1 teaspoon Asian toasted sesame oil

1 teaspoon sugar

¹/₄ teaspoon freshly ground white pepper

30 small (less than 2 inches across) hard-shell clams, scrubbed, or 1 pound medium shrimp, peeled and deveined, or 1 pound bay or sea scallops, or 1¹/₂ pounds squid, cleaned and cut into ¹/₂-inch rings

3 tablespoons peanut oil

3 tablespoons grated fresh ginger

2 small jalapeño chilies or 1 larger hot green chili, seeded, deveined (wear rubber gloves), and cut crosswise into thin strips

1 heaped tablespoon minced garlic

2 tablespoons dried fermented black beans, rinsed well and drained

2 scallions, both white and green parts, thinly sliced

In a small bowl, dissolve the cornstarch in the water and stir in the oyster sauce, soy sauce, sesame oil, sugar, and pepper. Set aside.

In a steamer over high heat, steam the clams for 4 to 6 minutes or until they begin to open. With a slotted spoon, transfer them as they open to a large bowl, discarding any unopened clams.

In a wok or large sauté pan over high heat, heat the oil until it just begins to smoke. Add the ginger, chilies, garlic, and black beans and stir-fry until the garlic is just golden, about 30 seconds. Add the clams and stir-fry just to coat the clams well with the black bean mixture. Pour the reserved oyster sauce mixture into the center of the wok or pan and bring the mixture to a boil, stirring until all the clams are coated well with the sauce.

Transfer the clams and sauce to a serving dish and sprinkle with the scallions. Serve with boiled rice.

Cannellini, Calamari, and Spinach Stew

SERVES 4

Squid is a seafood favorite in Italy, especially stewed or stuffed. But even in Italy many recipes for squid call for long cooking, which we find toughens seafood. We prefer to sauté squid quickly, just enough to turn it white and let it absorb flavors from the oil and vegetables it's cooked in. Then we add the other ingredients like the spinach and beans and let them cook just until wilted and heated through. This way the squid stays moist and tender. We stir in the garlic at the end of the cooking time to keep it pungent and fragrant—flavor that would be lost if cooked.

1/4 cup olive oil

1 carrot, minced

1 small onion, minced

1 celery rib, minced

1 pound cleaned squid, cut into 1/2-inch rings, the longer tentacles cut into 1-inch lengths

1 pound fresh spinach

1/2 cup homemade or canned tomato sauce

1/4 cup dry red or white wine

1/8 teaspoon cayenne pepper or 1/4 teaspoon hot red pepper flakes

1/2 teaspoon salt or to taste

1/2 teaspoon freshly ground black pepper

1 15-ounce can cannellini, drained and rinsed

1 large garlic clove, minced

In a large sauté pan or saucepan over moderate heat, bring the oil to rippling. Add the carrot, onion, and celery and cook, stirring occasionally, for 5 minutes or until the vegetables are soft and golden. Stir the squid into the vegetable mixture and cook for 2 or 3 minutes or until the squid turns white. Add the spinach and cook until just wilted, about 2 minutes.

Stir in the tomato sauce, wine, cayenne, salt, and pepper and cook for 3 minutes more. Add the beans and garlic and cook, stirring, for 2 minutes more or until the beans are just heated through.

Serve with warm crusty peasant bread to sop up the juices.

Scallops with Cannellini in a Gingery Tomato Sauce

SERVES 4

This is a very fresh-tasting and very quick (20 minutes start to finish) all-in-one main dish. Scallops should be cooked very briefly, or they tend to toughen—heat them just until they lose their translucent look and turn white. We even like to eat them raw—moist and shiny and smelling like an ocean breeze. To cook scallops, rinse them under cold water and pat dry with paper towels, sprinkle them with a little flour if you like, and sear them over high heat, barely a minute on each side if they are large sea scallops—one minute total, stirring, for tiny bay scallops.

In a large sauté pan over high heat, bring the oil to rippling and stir in half the garlic. Almost immediately, add the scallops and cook for 1 minute on each side. Remove the pan from the heat and transfer the scallops to a plate with a slotted spoon; set aside.

Return the pan to the heat and cook the onion, stirring, until softened, about 5 minutes. Add the ginger and cook the mixture, stirring, for 1 minute more.

Add the tomatoes and their juice, turn the heat down to simmer, and cook the sauce, stirring occasionally, for 5 to 8 minutes or until it thickens slightly. Season with salt and a generous amount of pepper.

Stir the beans into the tomato sauce and cook just until heated through. Just before serving, return the scallops to the pan along with the remaining garlic, stir once or twice, and transfer to a warm serving platter or bowl. Sprinkle with the parsley and serve with a salad and some good bread.

2 tablespoons canola or vegetable oil

2 large garlic cloves, minced

1½ pounds sea scallops, rinsed and patted dry

1 medium onion, finely chopped

1 tablespoon grated peeled fresh ginger

1 35-ounce can Italian tomatoes, chopped, with their liquid

salt and freshly ground pepper to taste

1 15-ounce can cannellini, drained and rinsed

¼ cup minced fresh parsley

Chickpea, Rosemary, and Sun-Dried Tomato Pita Pizzas

SERVES 6 AS A LUNCH OR SUPPER MAIN COURSE OR
10 TO 12 AS AN HORS D'OEUVRE OR SNACK

Don't pick up the phone! Don't call your local Piece-a-Pizza! Make your own pita pizza at home. Just split open and divide packaged pita breads horizontally so you have two circles, spread each side with our chickpea puree and its sun-dried tomato topping, and see if you ever go back to commercial pizzas. This one is wonderfully aromatic, slightly spicy, and completely different from any pizza you've ever eaten. Try it, then see the note at the end of the recipe for more ideas. You can offer pita pizzas as an hors d'oeuvre, a main course, or a snack. What a nice reinvention!

1/4 cup olive oil

2 large garlic cloves, thinly sliced

1 tablespoon minced fresh rosemary leaves

1/2 teaspoon hot red pepper flakes

1/2 teaspoon freshly ground pepper

1 19-ounce can chickpeas, drained and rinsed

1/2 teaspoon salt or to taste

3 6-inch pita breads, halved horizontally to form 6 rounds

6 ounces sun-dried tomatoes packed in oil, drained and finely chopped

1/2 cup freshly grated Parmesan cheese (about 2 ounces)

Preheat the oven to 400°.

In a large skillet or sauté pan over moderate heat, bring the oil to rippling. Add the garlic, rosemary, red pepper flakes, and black pepper and cook, stirring, until the garlic is pale golden, about 1 minute. Add the chickpeas and cook the mixture, stirring, until the chickpeas are hot and well coated with the oil and seasonings, about 2 minutes more.

Transfer the chickpea mixture and any oil in the pan to a food processor, add the salt, and blend the mixture until smooth.

Spread the inside surface (the rough side) of the pita rounds with the chickpea puree and sprinkle with the sun-dried tomatoes and Parmesan.

Arrange the pita pizzas on a large baking sheet and bake in the middle of the oven for 10 minutes or until the edges are crisp and golden. Serve the individual pita pizzas whole as an entree or cut into thin wedges as an hors d'oeuvre.

Variations: Spread the split pitas with something from the "Bread Spreads" chapter, add a topping of your choice (tomatoes, broccoli rabe, olives, shrimp, chicken, sausage, cheese, whatever is compatible), and pop into a 400° oven. In 10 minutes, less time than it takes a pizza-parlor-swifty to deliver the goods, you can serve up hot and bubbly made-to-order pizzas straight from your oven with a thin, crispy crust and the best toppings your family and friends have ever tasted.

Cannellini with Lemon and Basil over Penne

SERVES 4

Because this dish is so effortless and quickly tossed together, you may be surprised at its lively yet delicate flavor. Lemon and lemon zest lend a pleasant tartness to the slightly garlicky beans, while the basil and parsley add a garden-fresh minty taste. The dish is made with just these few ingredients, but each asserts its own distinct personality.

1 pound penne or other short tubular pasta

2 tablespoons olive oil

1 large garlic clove, minced

1 15-ounce can cannellini, drained and rinsed

1 lemon, the zest removed and julienned, the juice (about 2 tablespoons) reserved

1/2 cup shredded fresh basil leaves

1/2 cup chopped fresh parsley, preferably flat-leaf

1/2 teaspoon freshly ground pepper or more to taste

salt to taste

1/2 cup low-fat plain yogurt

freshly grated Parmesan cheese for serving

Bring a large kettle of salted water to a boil over high heat and add the penne. Cook for about 8 minutes, until al dente, while you prepare the sauce.

In a large skillet or sauté pan over moderate heat, bring the oil to rippling. Add the garlic and sauté until it is just golden, about 1 minute. Add the beans, lemon zest and juice, basil, parsley, pepper, and salt. Toss gently and let the mixture heat through for about 2 or 3 minutes. Reduce the heat to low and keep warm until the pasta is almost cooked.

Just before draining the pasta, stir the yogurt into the bean mixture. Drain the pasta in a colander and add it to the sauce, toss to coat well, and transfer to a serving bowl. Serve, passing the Parmesan at the table.

Note: Heavy cream, crème fraîche, or sour cream can stand in for the yogurt

Cranberry Beans Smothered in Herbs, Prosciutto, and Peppers

SERVES 4

When you read this recipe, you might think that the large amount of fresh herbs called for is a mistake. It isn't! Taste it and your mouth will tell you immediately that the amount is just right. The cranberry bean is an Italian favorite that's the complete reverse in color scheme from the American pinto bean: it has beige markings on a pink skin instead of pink markings on a beige skin. They're interchangeable.

2 tablespoons olive oil

1 medium red onion, finely chopped

2 large garlic cloves, thinly sliced

salt to taste

1 teaspoon freshly ground pepper

2 yellow bell peppers, seeded, deveined, and finely chopped

1 7-ounce jar roasted red peppers, drained and finely chopped

$1/2$ pound prosciutto or other cured ham, finely chopped

2 15-ounce cans cranberry or pinto beans, drained and rinsed

$1/2$ cup firmly packed chopped fresh basil leaves

$1/2$ cup firmly packed chopped fresh flat-leaf parsley

$1/2$ cup firmly packed chopped mixed fresh herbs such as marjoram, oregano, mint, cilantro, etc.

$1/2$ lemon

freshly grated Parmesan cheese for serving

In a medium sauté pan over moderate heat, bring the oil to rippling. Add the onion, garlic, salt, pepper, and yellow peppers and cook, stirring, until the vegetables are softened, about 5 minutes. Add the red peppers, prosciutto, and cranberry beans, stirring gently until combined and heated through.

Fold in all the herbs and transfer the mixture to a serving bowl. Squeeze the lemon juice over the beans and serve, passing the Parmesan cheese at the table.

Cranberry Bean, Lemon, and Olive Sauce over Chicken Breast Fillets

SERVES 4

Sauces thickened with bean puree rather than cornstarch or flour offer two bonuses: flavor and nutrition. This one also offers a little color—pink—which combines well with the green of the olives, their bright red pimiento stuffing, and the yellow of the lemon slices. The seasoning is also a little unusual, blending garlic, cumin, and cinnamon in a slightly Mexican manner. We usually serve this with steamed rice to absorb the sauce—the rice sprinkled with minced parsley to add even more color.

2 tablespoons olive oil

2 whole skinless, boneless
   chicken breasts, cut in half

salt and freshly ground
   pepper to taste

1 large yellow onion, chopped

1 heaped tablespoon minced
   garlic

4 flat anchovy fillets, chopped

1 teaspoon ground cumin or
   more to taste

1 teaspoon ground cinnamon

1 15-ounce can cranberry
   beans, drained and rinsed

$^1/_2$ cup fresh lemon juice

1 cup chicken broth

16 large pimiento-stuffed
   olives, sliced

8 lemon slices

In a large sauté pan or skillet over moderately high heat, bring the oil to rippling. Season the chicken breast halves with salt and pepper and add them to the pan one at a time, searing them until they just turn white, about 30 seconds on each side. Transfer them to a plate and set aside.

Add the onion to the sauté pan, reduce the heat to moderately low, and cook, stirring often, until the onion is softened, about 5 minutes. Add the garlic, anchovies, cumin, and cinnamon and cook the mixture, stirring, for 2 minutes or until the anchovies dissolve and the garlic just turns golden.

Meanwhile, puree the beans with the lemon juice in a blender or food processor until they are very smooth.

Return the chicken breasts to the pan and stir in the bean puree, chicken broth, olives, and lemon slices. Bring the liquid to a boil, reduce the heat to simmer, and cook, covered, for 7 to 10 minutes or until the chicken breasts are cooked through. Serve immediately, allowing one chicken breast half garnished with 2 lemon slices per portion, napping each breast with some of the sauce.

Lentils with Carrots, Ginger, and Pasta

SERVES 4

Recipes like this owe nothing to Italian cuisine except the pasta. Pasta in this case is merely a support vehicle, just as it is for myriad sauces and gravies. This time the sauce combines lentils with carrots and ginger. The last two ingredients are like a romance that's fated—the flavors meld in the most endearing manner. The love triangle is completed with the lentils. No rivalry here—simply a perfect ménage à trois.

In a large skillet over moderate heat, bring the oil to rippling and in it cook the onion with the thyme, stirring often, until the onion is nicely golden, about 15 minutes.

Meanwhile, combine the lentils with the water in a saucepan over high heat and bring to a boil. Reduce the heat to simmer and cook the lentils, covered, for 12 minutes. Add the carrots and ginger and simmer, covered, for 3 minutes more or until the lentils and carrots are just tender.

Transfer the lentil mixture with its liquid to the onions in the skillet, season with salt and pepper, stir, reduce the heat to moderately low, and simmer while you cook the pasta.

In a large saucepan of boiling salted water, cook the pasta until it is al dente, about 6 to 8 minutes. Drain, reserving a few tablespoons of the water, and stir the pasta into the lentil mixture. Toss to combine well, adding some of the pasta liquid if necessary.

Stir in the parsley and transfer the mixture to a heated serving bowl.

3 tablespoons olive oil

1 large yellow onion, finely chopped

1/2 teaspoon dried thyme, crushed

3/4 cup lentils

2 1/2 cups water

2 carrots, finely chopped

2 tablespoons finely grated fresh ginger

salt and freshly ground pepper to taste

1 pound small pasta shapes such as rotelle or small bow ties

1/2 cup minced fresh parsley leaves

Savory Lentils with Spinach and Tomatoes over Penne

SERVES 4

Italian cooks often use lentils to sauce pasta. This is an especially healthful and abundantly flavorful combination that is effortless to prepare. Just a bowlful reveals why lentils were a prized part of the Roman legions' diet, sustaining them as they lusted after territories to enlarge their empire. First cultivated in southwestern Asia more than 10,000 years ago, they—along with garlic and onions—later fueled the builders of Egypt's pyramids. Lentils have an illustrious history, and this dish, combining several of those ancient ingredients and more, continues a culinary tradition.

2 tablespoons olive oil

1 medium onion, coarsely
 chopped

4 large garlic cloves, minced

²/₃ cup lentils

1 cup chicken broth

¹/₂ cup water

1 teaspoon Italian seasoning,
 crumbled

¹/₄ teaspoon dried oregano,
 crumbled

¹/₂ teaspoon hot red pepper
 flakes or to taste

1 14- to 16-ounce can whole
 tomatoes with their juice

1 tablespoon ketchup

salt and freshly ground
 pepper to taste

1 10-ounce package chopped
 frozen spinach or 1 pound
 fresh, chopped

1 pound penne or other short
 tubular pasta

freshly grated Parmesan
 cheese for serving

In a large saucepan or sauté pan set over moderately high heat, bring the oil to rippling. Add the onion and garlic and cook, stirring, until the onion is softened, about 5 minutes. Stir in the lentils, broth, water, Italian seasoning, oregano, and red pepper flakes, bring to a boil, reduce the heat to simmer, and cook for 10 minutes. Add the tomatoes, ketchup, salt, and pepper and simmer, breaking up the tomatoes with a wooden spoon, for 10 minutes. Add the spinach and cook until tender, about 2 minutes.

Meanwhile, bring a large kettle of salted water to a boil and, about 10 minutes before the sauce is finished, add the penne and cook for about 8 minutes or until al dente. Drain the pasta in a colander and add it to the sauce, toss to coat well, transfer to a decorative bowl, and serve, passing the Parmesan at the table.

Lima Beans with Shrimp, Tomatoes, and Ricotta Salata

SERVES 4

There is a certain earthy quality about lima beans that makes people love them or hate them—no one seems neutral. If you're not crazy about limas, try them this way, and you might be converted. Or substitute any other bean you like—chickpeas, large cannellini, or favas work well because of their size. A salad of greens and sliced endive with a simple vinaigrette dressing, some dense peasant bread, and you have a satisfying meal.

In a large sauté pan over moderate heat, bring 2 tablespoons of the oil to rippling and in it cook the garlic and tomatoes, stirring occasionally, for 15 to 20 minutes, until the tomato sauce has thickened. Season with salt and pepper.

In a large skillet over moderately high heat, bring the remaining tablespoon of oil to rippling and in it sauté the shrimp, stirring, for 1 minute. Add the wine and deglaze the skillet, scraping up the brown bits.

Add the shrimp mixture to the tomato sauce along with the ricotta salata, lima beans, and more salt and pepper. Simmer the mixture for 3 minutes or until the shrimp are cooked through. Sprinkle with the parsley and serve.

3 tablespoons olive oil

3 large garlic cloves, minced

3 red ripe tomatoes (about 1$^1\!/_2$ pounds), peeled and finely chopped

salt and freshly ground pepper to taste

1 pound medium shrimp, peeled

$^1\!/_4$ cup dry white wine

$^1\!/_4$ pound ricotta salata (available at Italian grocery stores, specialty food stores, and some supermarkets) or feta cheese, finely crumbled

1 10-ounce package frozen lima beans, thawed

2 tablespoons minced fresh parsley leaves

Pigeon Peas with Mustard Greens, Garlic, and Pasta Shells

SERVES 4

Pigeon peas (gandules) and mustard greens are rarely used in American kitchens, except in the South, and especially not in a dish with Italian cooking techniques like this one. But the mustard greens lend the kind of bite (heat) that Italians cherish, the pigeon peas and tomatoes a pretty color scheme, and the pasta additional substance—the result more Little Italy than Old South. Canned pigeon peas are found in the Hispanic section of supermarkets and at many health food stores.

2 tablespoons basil-flavored oil or olive oil

¼ teaspoon hot red pepper flakes or more to taste

6 large garlic cloves, thinly sliced

2 pounds mustard greens, stems discarded and leaves finely shredded

salt and freshly ground pepper to taste

¼ cup water

2 cups drained canned tomatoes, juice reserved and tomatoes chopped

1 15-ounce can pigeon peas, drained and rinsed

¾ pound medium shells or other medium pasta shape

¼ cup freshly grated Parmesan cheese, plus more for serving

In a large sauté pan over moderately high heat, bring the oil to rippling. Add the red pepper flakes and cook, stirring, for a few seconds. Turn the heat down to moderate and cook the garlic, stirring, until it is just golden, about 1 minute. Add the mustard greens, salt, pepper, and water and cook, covered, for 5 minutes or until the greens are just wilted.

Add the tomatoes and their juice and the pigeon peas, stirring to combine, and cook, covered, for 3 minutes more or until the greens are tender.

Meanwhile, in a kettle of boiling salted water boil the shells until they are al dente, about 8 minutes. Drain the pasta in a colander and add to the cooked bean–mustard green mixture. Toss with the ¼ cup of Parmesan cheese.

Transfer to a serving bowl or to plates and serve, passing additional Parmesan at the table.

Note: If basil-flavored oil is not available, you can substitute 1 tablespoon chopped fresh basil leaves and add them along with the tomatoes and pigeon peas.

Pink Beans with Chicken Breasts, Oranges, and Walnuts

Skinless, boneless chicken breasts are so quick cooking that we always seem to have some on hand for a thrown-together one-dish meal. With Sally at the stove, however, nothing ever tastes thrown together. What we have within arm's reach is usually the inspiration. This dish came to her out of the blue one night (and the fridge, fruit bowl, and pantry), and was so delicious we decided to include it here.

In a large sauté pan or skillet over moderately high heat, bring the oil to rippling. Add the chicken seasoned with salt and pepper and cook, stirring, until it just turns white, about 1 minute. With a slotted spoon, transfer the chicken to a plate and set aside.

In the oil remaining in the pan, cook the onions, stirring, until golden, about 5 minutes. Reduce the heat to moderate and stir in the orange juice, broth, sherry, cinnamon, cardamom, cloves, and raisins and simmer, covered, for 10 minutes. Add the beans and simmer, covered, for 2 minutes more. Add the reserved chicken pieces, walnuts, and orange sections and cook for another 5 minutes or until the chicken is just tender.

Taste for seasoning and add more salt and pepper if necessary. With a fork, mash some of the beans and stir to thicken the gravy. Sprinkle with the scallions and serve.

2 tablespoons olive oil

2 whole skinless, boneless chicken breasts, cut into bite-size pieces

salt and freshly ground pepper to taste

2 medium onions, finely chopped

1 cup fresh orange juice

1 cup chicken broth

2 tablespoons medium-dry sherry

½ teaspoon ground cinnamon

¼ teaspoon ground cardamom

⅛ teaspoon ground cloves

½ cup raisins

1 15-ounce can pink beans, drained and rinsed

½ cup walnut pieces

2 navel oranges, peeled, the sections cut free from the membranes

2 tablespoons thinly sliced scallion greens

Pinto Beans with Sautéed Zucchini, Basil, and Anchovies

SERVES 4

Zucchini contains lots of water. If it is julienned or shredded and salted, then allowed to stand for about 10 minutes or more, much of the moisture will seep out, and it will sauté crisp instead of becoming wilted from inadvertent steaming. Combined with the beans, basil, anchovies, and garlic, the resulting contrast in textures (soft and crunchy) and flavors (bland and zingy) is lively if not giddy. A plateful can easily be a meal because each forkful seduces the diner into scooping up the next. Add good bread and a salad, and you can satisfy any trencherman.

6 medium zucchini (about
    1¹/₂ to 2 pounds)

2 teaspoons salt

¹/₃ cup packed shredded fresh
    basil leaves or more to
    taste

¹/₂ cup olive oil

¹/₂ teaspoon hot red pepper
    flakes

2 tablespoons finely chopped
    garlic

4 canned flat anchovies,
    chopped

1 teaspoon freshly ground
    black pepper or more to
    taste

2 15-ounce cans pinto beans,
    drained and rinsed

freshly grated Parmesan
    cheese or crisp Chinese
    fried noodles for garnish if
    desired

In a food processor fitted with the fine-shredding blade or with a hand grater, shred the zucchini. Transfer to a sieve or a colander, sprinkle with the salt, toss to mix well, and let drain for 10 minutes or more. By small handfuls, squeeze the drained zucchini to extract even more liquid. Combine the squeezed zucchini with the basil in a mixing bowl, mixing well.

In a large skillet or sauté pan over moderately high heat, bring the oil to rippling. Add the red pepper flakes, garlic, and anchovies and cook, stirring, until the garlic just begins to color and the anchovies dissolve into the oil, about 1 minute. Toss in the zucchini-basil mixture, add black pepper, and sauté, stirring often, until the zucchini turns a nice golden color, about 4 to 5 minutes. Add the pinto beans and gently fold them into the zucchini mixture. Heat the beans through, mixing gently and carefully once or twice, for about 2 minutes.

Serve with grated Parmesan cheese or a sprinkling of fried Chinese noodles.

Red Beans with Anchovy and Green Olive Sauce

SERVES 4

We have made this sauce for spaghetti, calamari, clams, and artichokes. It's delicious with each of them. But it's even better with beans. In this recipe we suggest red beans as the base, but you could substitute black beans, black-eyed peas, cannellini, or chickpeas. You can also fortify and extend this dish with calamari sautéed briefly in the garlic before adding the anchovies—or drained canned baby whole clams or mussels, or a drained can of white tuna, flaked, added when you toss in the beans and cooked just long enough to heat through. As you can see, it's a very adaptable sauce.

In a large heavy skillet over moderate heat, bring the oil to rippling. Add the garlic and sauté, stirring, until pale golden, about 1 minute. Add the anchovies and cook, stirring and mashing, until the anchovies are dissolved, about 1 minute. Stir in the black pepper, red pepper flakes, and Italian seasoning and cook, stirring, for 1 minute more. Add the olives, parsley, and red beans and cook, stirring gently, until heated through and completely coated with the sauce, about 2 minutes.

If necessary, add up to ¹/₂ cup chicken or clam broth to thin the sauce to the desired consistency. Serve immediately.

Note: This dish can be served all by itself or on steamed white rice.

If you add the rice or any of the other earlier suggestions, the recipe can be stretched to serve 6 or 8.

¹/₃ cup olive oil

6 large garlic cloves, thinly sliced

1 2-ounce can flat anchovies, drained, patted dry, and chopped

¹/₂ teaspoon freshly ground black pepper or more to taste

¹/₄ teaspoon hot red pepper flakes or 2 dashes of Tabasco sauce

1 teaspoon Italian seasoning, crumbled

³/₄ cup pimiento-stuffed olives, finely chopped

¹/₂ cup finely chopped flat-leaf parsley

2 15-ounce cans red beans, drained and rinsed

¹/₂ cup hot chicken broth or bottled clam juice if needed

Red Beans with Browned Bits of Pork in Peanut Sauce

SERVES 4 TO 6

You might think, because of the peanut butter and sesame oil sauce, the inspiration for this dish is the Chinese appetizer cold sesame noodles. But the resemblance is slight, and rather than noodles we use beans. The dish is served hot, and nicely browned ground pork is its base. If pork isn't part of your diet, by all means substitute julienned chicken breasts, ground beef, or turkey. It works with all three (with a slight adjustment in the cooking time), so it's a good recipe to have in your repertoire. It also can be made with leftovers like steak, turkey, or any grilled or roasted meat from another meal, finely chopped and sautéed briefly just to brown it.

1 tablespoon vegetable oil

1 pound ground pork

4 teaspoons sugar

2 large garlic cloves, minced

1 tablespoon minced fresh ginger

1/4 cup light soy sauce

1/2 teaspoon hot red pepper flakes

3 tablespoons fresh lemon juice

2 teaspoons sesame oil (preferably Asian toasted)

2/3 cup smooth peanut butter

1 cup hot water

2 15-ounce cans red beans, drained and rinsed

1 cup thinly sliced scallions, both white and green parts

1 small cucumber (preferably Kirby), diced

In a heavy skillet or sauté pan over moderate heat, bring the oil to rippling. Add the pork and cook, stirring and breaking up the lumps, until it is no longer pink, about 5 minutes. Pour off all but 2 tablespoons of fat.

Add 2 teaspoons of the sugar, the garlic, ginger, 1 tablespoon of the soy sauce, and the red pepper flakes to the pork, increase the heat to high, and sauté the mixture, stirring occasionally, until the pork is browned well, about 5 minutes more.

Meanwhile, in a blender or food processor, blend together the remaining soy sauce, the lemon juice, sesame oil, peanut butter, and enough hot water to thin the sauce to heavy cream consistency.

Add the beans to the pork mixture in the pan and stir for about 2 minutes to combine and heat through. Remove the pan from the heat and toss the mixture with the peanut sauce.

Spoon onto a warm serving dish and sprinkle with the scallions and cucumber. Serve hot.

Sugar Snap Peas and Penne with Radish Greens Pesto

SERVES 4

The sugar snap pea is a relative newcomer to the produce world, a talented starlet about to be elevated to star status. As with real starlets, it takes a good script (read: recipe) and seasoned performers to put her in the best setting. Here sugar snap peas are combined with penne, the quill-shaped pasta, and a starlet-manqué, radish greens. Have you, like us, always thrown them away? Don't. They're not only wonderful in salads and to add zing to soups, but their tongue-stinging flavor is a revelation in our pestolike sauce that dramatically emphasizes the sweetness of the peas and perks up the bland, tender-textured macaroni. Or use radicchio, collard greens, or mustard greens, all of which have a pleasant bite but are rarely destined for pesto.

In a food processor, combine the radish greens, walnuts, Parmesan, 1 teaspoon or more salt, and the garlic and pulse, scraping down the sides occasionally, until the walnuts are finely chopped. With the motor running, add the oil in dribbles and process the pesto until it is smooth (add a little more oil if necessary). Set aside.

In a large saucepan of boiling salted water, blanch the sugar snap peas for 30 to 45 seconds, until they are just crisp-tender; don't overcook them. Remove them immediately with a slotted spoon or skimmer to a large serving bowl and toss them with half of the pesto.

In the same boiling water, cook the penne until it is al dente, about 8 to 10 minutes. Drain the pasta, reserving $1/2$ cup of the cooking liquid, and toss the penne in the bowl with the peas, the reserved cooking liquid, and the remaining pesto. Add salt and pepper and serve immediately.

greens from 1 bunch of red radishes (about 3 or 4 cups)

$3/4$ cup walnut or raw cashew pieces

$1/2$ cup freshly grated Parmesan cheese

salt to taste

2 large garlic cloves

2 tablespoons olive oil

$1/2$ pound sugar snap peas

1 pound penne or other short tubular pasta

freshly ground pepper to taste

Creamy Black and White Beans with Clams, Scallops, and Shrimp

SERVES 4 TO 6

We're partial to risotto, especially the seafood risotto of Venice. Of course, beans can't stand in for Italian rice (like they can for pasta), but we've discovered that they can offer a result that's, as they say, "the same but different."

2 tablespoons unsalted butter

1 medium onion, finely chopped

1 small fennel bulb (about 1/2 pound), finely chopped

1 tablespoon minced garlic

1 10-ounce can black beans, drained and rinsed

1 15-ounce can small cannellini, drained and rinsed

1/2 cup dry white wine

1/4 teaspoon ground turmeric

2 tablespoons olive oil

1 large garlic clove, thinly sliced

1 pound large shrimp (about 20), peeled, deveined if desired, each cut into thirds

1/2 pound bay scallops

1 10-ounce can whole baby clams, drained, the liquor reserved

2 tablespoons Pernod or other anise-flavored liqueur

2 tablespoons minced fresh flat-leaf parsley leaves

salt and freshly ground pepper to taste

In a sauté pan over moderate heat, bring the butter to foaming. When the foam subsides, sauté the onion, fennel, and minced garlic, stirring occasionally, until the onion and fennel are softened, about 3 to 5 minutes. Stir in the black beans and half the cannellini and cook, stirring, for 2 minutes.

Puree the remaining cannellini in a food processor or blender and stir into the bean mixture. Add the white wine and turmeric and cook, stirring, for 3 minutes more. Turn down the heat to moderately low while the seafood is stir-fried.

In a skillet set over high heat, bring the oil to rippling and in it sauté the sliced garlic, shrimp, and scallops, stirring, for 1 minute. Stir in the clams and 2 tablespoons of the reserved clam liquor and cook, stirring, until the clams are just heated through, about 30 seconds.

Stir the seafood mixture into the bean mixture, increase the heat to moderate, and cook, stirring, for 2 minutes. Add the Pernod and cook the seafood/bean mixture, stirring, for 1 minute more.

Remove the pan from the heat and stir in the parsley, salt, and pepper. Serve immediately.

Three-Bean, Shrimp, and Vegetable Potpourri

SERVES 4 TO 6

We like one-dish meals. Less cleanup and fewer pots on the stove in our tiny kitchen. This recipe started off as a soup but was so flavorful and filling that we soon cut back on the liquid and served it as a main course over rice. The brown beans are a nod to the recipe's Scandinavian origin. If you can't find them, substitute black-eyed peas or red, black, white, lima, or pinto beans. The taste doesn't change—just the color.

1 large boiling potato, peeled, cut into ¼-inch dice, and reserved in a bowl under 2 cups cold water

2 carrots, thinly sliced

1 10-ounce package frozen peas

1 small head of cauliflower, broken into tiny florets

½ pound fresh green beans, cut into ½-inch pieces

½ pound spinach, coarse stems discarded, finely chopped

½ cup half-and-half

2 large egg yolks

½ pound shrimp, peeled and deveined

1 15-ounce can brown beans, drained and rinsed

1 teaspoon coarse salt or to taste

½ teaspoon freshly ground pepper or more to taste

1 tablespoon aquavit or dry sherry if desired

2 tablespoons snipped fresh dill

In a large saucepan over moderately high heat, bring to a boil the potato with its water, the carrots, peas, cauliflower, and green beans and cook for 7 minutes or until the vegetables are tender. Add the spinach and cook, stirring, for 1 minute more.

In a small bowl, whisk together the half-and-half and egg yolks. Stir about 1 cup of the hot vegetable mixture into the yolks a little at a time (so as not to cook the yolks). Gradually stir the yolk mixture back into the vegetable mixture.

Reduce the heat to simmer and cook (do not boil) the mixture, stirring, for 1 minute. Add the shrimp, brown beans, salt, and pepper and cook for 2 minutes or until the shrimp are pink and just firm and the beans have heated through.

Stir in the aquavit and serve with steamed rice. Garnish with snipped dill.

MAIN
COURSES

Black and White Beans
with Mussels in Arugula Cream Sauce

The Italian pasta dish paglia e fieno *inspired this dish. It mingles strands of yellow and green pasta to form a colorful palette on which to mix a cream sauce of ham, peas, and, perhaps, mushrooms. We've changed the color scheme here, opting for the dramatic chiaroscuro effect of black and white beans combined with the gray/beige of mussels in a cream sauce dappled with the deep green of arugula.*

In a heavy skillet or sauté pan over moderately high heat, bring the oil to rippling, reduce the heat to moderately low, and cook the onion, stirring, until it is softened, about 5 minutes. Add the wine, clam juice, and water, increase the heat to high, and bring the mixture to a boil.

Add the mussels and steam them, covered, for 2 minutes or until they are opened. Transfer them with tongs to a bowl, discarding any that are unopened. Let the mussels cool for a few minutes until they can be handled and remove them from their shells, discarding the shells.

Let the liquid remaining in the skillet continue to boil until it has been reduced to about 1 cup, add the cream, reduce the heat to simmer, and cook the mixture for about 3 minutes or until it is thickened.

Add the arugula, the mussels and any liquid accumulated in the bowl, and salt and pepper. Stir in the black and white beans and continue to cook for 2 minutes more or until the arugula is wilted and the beans are heated through.

2 tablespoons olive oil

1 medium onion, chopped

$1/2$ cup dry white wine

$1/2$ cup bottled clam juice

$1/2$ cup water

3 dozen mussels, scrubbed and debearded

$1/2$ cup heavy cream

2 bunches of arugula, coarse stems discarded, coarsely chopped (about 3 cups)

salt and freshly ground pepper to taste

1 15-ounce can black beans, drained and rinsed

1 15-ounce can white beans, drained and rinsed

Black Bean and Chicken Pancakes with Gazpacho-Yogurt Sauce

SERVES 4

These pancakes, fragrant with cumin and cilantro, can be topped with our sauce recommendation, your favorite salsa, or a savory chutney. Substitute cooked sausage, ham, turkey, pot roast, or whatever you discover—even vegetables—for the chicken.

2 15-ounce cans black beans, drained and rinsed

1 cup shredded cooked chicken

2 teaspoons salt

1 canned pickled jalapeño chili, finely chopped

$1/2$ cup minced cilantro or parsley leaves

1 large egg, beaten lightly

$1/2$ cup dry bread crumbs

$1/4$ cup canola or vegetable oil

1 large ripe tomato, finely chopped

2 large garlic cloves, minced

1 small cucumber (preferably Kirby), unpeeled, finely chopped

1 red or yellow bell pepper, seeded, deveined, and finely chopped

1 small onion, finely chopped

1 teaspoon red wine vinegar

$1/2$ teaspoon freshly ground black pepper

1 cup regular, low-fat, or nonfat plain yogurt

In a food processor, pulse the beans until they are a coarse puree. Transfer to a bowl and stir in the chicken, 1 teaspoon of the salt, the jalapeño, the cilantro, and the egg.

Scoop up $1/4$ cup of the mixture at a time into $1/2$-inch-thick cakes. Coat the cakes well with the bread crumbs, pressing them lightly into the surface.

In a sauté pan or large skillet over moderately high heat, bring the oil to rippling and sauté the pancakes, turning them once, for 4 to 5 minutes or until they are nicely browned and crisp. (If you are sautéing the pancakes in batches, transfer them as they are done to a baking sheet and keep warm in a 250° oven.)

Meanwhile, in a bowl, combine the rest of the ingredients, including the remaining teaspoon of salt.

Place 2 pancakes on each of 4 plates, top with some of the gazpacho-yogurt sauce, and serve, passing any remaining sauce at the table.

Black Beans and Shrimp with Four Anise Flavors

SERVES 4

The addition of Pernod or other anise-flavored liqueur to bouillabaisse is traditional. In fact, in Provence most fish stews are enlivened with this anise-flavored spirit. Keeping this in mind, we developed this recipe to utilize four different sources of this classic flavoring that so enhances seafood: Pernod, fennel bulb, fennel seed, and the beautiful green feathery fronds of the fennel plant. The black beans add substance and are a nice color foil for the pink shrimp, the pale, pale green of the fennel, and the vibrant emerald of the fresh fennel leaves. The perfect accompaniment is plain steamed white rice.

In a shallow glass baking dish, combine the wine, Pernod, lime juice, 1 teaspoon of the garlic, the fennel seeds, onion, and fennel bulb. Set aside to marinate briefly.

In a skillet over moderately high heat, bring the oil to rippling and in it sauté the remaining teaspoon of garlic for 10 seconds, stirring. Add the shrimp and sauté, stirring, for 2 minutes. With a slotted spoon, transfer the shrimp to a plate and set aside.

With the slotted spoon, transfer the vegetables to the skillet, reserving the marinade, and sauté them, stirring, for 5 minutes. Add the reserved marinade to the sautéed vegetables, reduce the heat to simmer, and cook the mixture, stirring occasionally, for 15 minutes or until the fennel is crisp-tender and the liquid has almost evaporated.

Add the shrimp with any accumulated juices, the black beans, salt, and pepper and cook for 2 to 4 minutes more or until the shrimp and beans are heated through.

Transfer the mixture to a warm serving platter and surround with the reserved fennel fronds.

1 cup dry white wine

2 tablespoons Pernod or other anise-flavored spirit such as Ricard or ouzo

1 tablespoon fresh lime juice

2 teaspoons minced garlic

2 teaspoons fennel seeds

1 small onion, finely chopped

1 medium or large fennel bulb, halved through the root and thinly sliced, reserving the green feathery fronds for garnish

1 tablespoon olive oil

1 pound medium shrimp, peeled and deveined

1 15-ounce can black beans, drained and rinsed

salt and freshly ground pepper to taste

Black Beans and Rice Pilaf with Pistachios and Raisins

SERVES 4

In this recipe India's basmati rice is blended with the Caribbean's black beans, the Middle East's pistachios and raisins, plus exotic spices like turmeric and aromatic cardamom—all brought together by a basically French technique for cooking rice to produce food that may speak in many tongues but translates into contentment for all.

3 tablespoons unsalted butter

1 medium onion, finely chopped

1 large garlic clove, minced

$1/2$ teaspoon ground turmeric

$1/2$ teaspoon ground cardamom

salt and freshly ground pepper to taste

1 cup basmati rice

1 15-ounce can black beans, drained and rinsed

$1^{1}/2$ cups hot chicken broth

3 tablespoons pistachio nuts, lightly toasted and chopped

3 tablespoons golden raisins, soaked in boiling water for 1 minute and drained

3 scallions, both white and green parts, thinly sliced

In a medium saucepan over moderate heat, bring 2 tablespoons of the butter to foaming. When the foam subsides, stir in the onion, garlic, turmeric, cardamom, salt, and pepper. Continue stirring until the onion has softened, about 5 minutes.

Add the rice to the butter mixture and cook it, stirring, until it has lost its opaque appearance and is coated with the butter, about 1 to 2 minutes.

Add the beans and $1/4$ cup of the broth and cook, stirring, until the broth has been absorbed. Add the remaining broth, bring the liquid to a boil over high heat, lower the heat to simmer, and cook, covered, for 17 minutes or until the liquid is absorbed and the rice is tender.

Stir in the pistachios, raisins, scallions, and the remaining tablespoon of butter. Taste for seasoning and add more salt and pepper if necessary. Mound on a warm serving platter and serve immediately.

Black-Eyed Peas with Swiss Chard

SERVES 4

Black-eyed peas were brought to this country by the slave traders, which leads most people to think they are native to Africa. Actually they are probably indigenous to China and were first transported to Arab traders and Africans via the Silk Route. By the eighteenth century they were an established part of the plantation diet. The famous southern dish hoppin' John is usually made with black-eyed peas, which supplanted the Caribbean pigeon peas (pois à pigeon in French, pronounced ah-pee-jon, which was transposed into American English as hoppin' John) that were in the original recipe. This dish is no relation. For a fast and flavorful supper, serve it along with a salad of sliced tomatoes sprinkled with chopped basil or parsley and a little lemon juice, or to make the dish even more filling fold in a quick-cooked small pasta shape like little bow ties or orzo. The original recipe also works as a hearty side dish.

Remove and discard the tough white stems from the Swiss chard and chop the greens coarsely.

In a large skillet or sauté pan over medium-high heat, bring the oil to rippling. Add the onion and sauté for 5 minutes or until it is soft and translucent. Add the Swiss chard and stir until it wilts, about 2 minutes.

Add the black-eyed peas, salt and pepper to taste, and Tabasco, stir to combine, and bring back to a simmer. Cook for about 2 minutes, stirring occasionally, to heat the beans and let them absorb some flavor. Taste for seasoning and serve immediately or cover and keep warm over very low heat.

1 pound Swiss chard

1 tablespoon olive oil

1 medium onion, chopped

2 15-ounce cans black-eyed peas, drained and rinsed

salt and freshly ground pepper to taste

2 dashes Tabasco sauce or a pinch of cayenne pepper or $1/4$ teaspoon hot red pepper flakes

Cannellini with Garlic-Sautéed Watercress and Chicken

SERVES 4

Like arugula, watercress is one of those greens that find their way into salads but not often into cooked dishes. We love their spicy flavor, especially when combined with canned beans and boneless chicken breasts in a quick sauté. This dish could be assembled and cooked in less than 5 minutes if it weren't for the time it takes to peel and mince the garlic and cut up the chicken. But if you're quick with the chef's knife, it could be on the table in 10 minutes flat. So little time for such spirited flavor.

2 tablespoons olive oil or good-quality canola oil

4 large garlic cloves, minced

1 skinless, boneless chicken breast, cut into bite-size pieces

1/2 teaspoon freshly ground pepper

2 bunches of watercress, rinsed but not dried, coarse stems discarded

1 19-ounce can small cannellini drained and rinsed

salt to taste

In a large sauté pan over moderately high heat, bring the oil to rippling and in it sauté three quarters of the garlic with the chicken pieces and pepper for about 3 minutes or until the garlic is fragrant and the chicken is opaque. Add the watercress with the water clinging to it, stirring to combine well, and sauté, covered, for 2 minutes more. Add the cannellini, stirring gently, season with salt, and heat through for about 1 minute.

Sprinkle the mixture with the remaining garlic, toss quickly, transfer to a warm serving bowl, and serve.

Cool and Creamy Lentil Salsa Under Hot Grilled Fish Fillets

SERVES 4

Lentils are a favorite of ours because they cook quickly right from the package. We use brown lentils here; to use red or green lentils, adjust the cooking times accordingly—red are quicker; green take 20 to 30 minutes. This is a lovely way to serve fish fillets, sitting elegantly astride the cool but spicy lentil salsa.

In a large saucepan over high heat, bring water to a boil and cook the lentils, uncovered, for 15 to 20 minutes or until just tender. Drain in a sieve and rinse under cold running water until cool.

In a bowl, toss the lentils with the bell pepper, jalapeño, onion, tomatoes, ¼ cup cilantro, the oil, vinegar, Maggi, yogurt, salt, and pepper.

Pat the fish fillets dry, sprinkle them with salt and pepper, and dredge them in the flour, shaking off the excess.

Oil a ridged grill pan or skillet set over moderately high heat and grill the fillets for 4 to 5 minutes on each side or until they just flake.

Pool an equal portion of the salsa on each of 4 plates and top each serving with a fillet. Sprinkle each fillet with the remaining cilantro and serve immediately.

¾ cup lentils

1 red bell pepper, seeded, deveined, and finely chopped

1 jalapeño chili, seeded, deveined (wear rubber gloves), and finely chopped

1 medium onion, finely chopped

2 ripe tomatoes, chopped

¼ cup firmly packed finely chopped cilantro leaves, plus 1 tablespoon for garnish

3 tablespoons olive oil plus more for oiling the pan

2 tablespoons red wine vinegar

3 dashes of Maggi seasoning

¼ cup plain yogurt

salt and freshly ground pepper to taste

4 skinless fish fillets: 6 to 8 ounces each red snapper, orange roughy, flounder, or similar mild-flavored fish

all-purpose flour for dredging the fillets

Chickpea Gnocchi with Gorgonzola Sauce

SERVES 6

Gnocchi are a popular alternative to pasta in Italy from Rome on up the boot, but especially in Tuscany, where beans are uncommonly common. Yet gnocchi are always made from semolina flour or potatoes, never beans. If Tuscans were to use beans, however, they'd probably choose cannellini, their favorite. Not to be perverse, but because they are drier and have a nuttier flavor than cooked white beans, we use chickpeas. Both these characteristics of chickpeas make them admirably suited to making gnocchi because the beans should have a flavor of their own and must dry out to make a tender, unsticky dumpling. We've doused them in a rich Gorgonzola sauce. You can substitute Roquefort if Gorgonzola isn't easy to come by in your neighborhood—a substitution that isn't traditional. But then again, neither are gnocchi fashioned from chickpeas.

1 19-ounce can chickpeas, drained, rinsed, and pureed

2 large garlic cloves, minced

salt and freshly ground white pepper to taste

¹/₄ teaspoon freshly grated nutmeg or more to taste

2 tablespoons minced flat-leaf parsley

1 cup plus 3 tablespoons all-purpose flour

2 tablespoons unsalted butter

1 cup milk

¹/₂ pound Gorgonzola cheese, crumbled

In a large kettle over high heat, bring about 1 gallon of salted water to a boil.

Meanwhile, in a saucepan over moderately low heat, heat the chickpea puree, stirring and beating it with a wooden spoon until no more steam rises from it, about 2 or 3 minutes. Beat in the garlic, salt, pepper, nutmeg, parsley, and 1 cup of the flour and continue beating until the mixture comes away from the sides of the saucepan and is very smooth and fluffy, about 3 or 4 minutes more.

Transfer the dough to a work surface spread with 1 tablespoon of the flour, flatten the dough with the back of the wooden spoon, and let it cool until it can be handled, about 5 minutes.

Cut the dough into several pieces and roll each piece into a cylinder about ¹/₂ inch in diameter. Cut each cylinder into 1-inch pieces. Press each piece with the tines of a fork to produce a grid effect.

Drop the gnocchi, all at once, into the kettle of boiling water. Gently stir the water with a wooden spoon and cook for 2 or 3 minutes or until the gnocchi rise to the surface.

With a slotted spoon, remove the gnocchi from the water to a buttered serving platter and cover with foil to keep warm.

To make the sauce, in a saucepan over moderate heat, bring the butter to foaming. When the foam subsides, add the remaining 2 tablespoons of flour, stirring for about 1 to 2 minutes (be careful not to let the mixture brown) to make a roux.

Whisk in the milk until the mixture is smooth and simmer until it thickens, about 3 minutes. Add the Gorgonzola and stir until it is incorporated but is still a little lumpy.

Pour the hot sauce over the gnocchi and serve immediately.

Chicken Breasts Ajillo with Red Beans

SERVES 4

Pollo ajillo is practically a national dish in Spain. You see it on almost every menu. Spanish cooks cut up a whole chicken, brown it in oil, then add the garlic and brandy and set it aflame. When the flames die down, they cover the chicken and cook it for about 15 minutes more. Using boned chicken breasts, as we do here, the dish takes less than 15 minutes to cook altogether. The red beans are a Mexican touch that makes this a one-dish meal with an especially appealing color scheme when served on turmeric- or saffron-tinted rice. The rice will take 20 minutes to cook, so start it before cooking the chicken. Note: Add a pinch of saffron or 1/2 teaspoon turmeric to the cooking water to make yellow rice.

¹/₄ cup olive oil

2 whole skinless, boneless chicken breasts, each cut in half

1 whole head of garlic, peeled and minced in the food processor

¹/₄ teaspoon freshly ground black pepper

¹/₄ teaspoon cayenne pepper

¹/₈ teaspoon sweet paprika

3 tablespoons brandy

¹/₄ cup chicken broth

1 19-ounce can red beans, drained and rinsed

coarse salt to taste

2 cups cooked yellow rice (see note above)

In a large sauté pan over moderate heat, bring the oil to rippling. Add the chicken breasts and garlic, reserving 1 tablespoon, and sauté, turning the breasts until they are just cooked through and golden, about 3 minutes. Sprinkle the breasts with the black pepper, cayenne, and paprika.

Add the brandy and standing well back, ignite the liquid and stir until the flames die down. Add the chicken broth and red beans, reduce the heat to simmer, cover, and cook for 3 minutes more. Sprinkle with the reserved garlic and salt. Transfer the chicken breasts to a serving dish that has been mounded with yellow rice. Spoon the beans and sauce over the chicken and serve.

White Beans and Peas with Brown Butter Sauce

This is a simple main dish that relies on dark brown butter for its unusual taste. There is something about butter that's cooked until it is almost burned that has intrigued cooks for centuries. One of our favorite dishes before calories and cholesterol came into our consciousness was brains in black butter. Brains, even more so than most organ meats, are almost solid cholesterol, so we decided to try substituting beans, which of course have no cholesterol and allow the butter, Parmesan, and yogurt to bear the burden of the forbidden. If you use nonfat yogurt, you can pare the fat down even further. Serve this as a main dish at a supper for 4 or as a side dish or first course at a dinner for 6 to 8.

In a heavy skillet or sauté pan over moderate heat, cook the butter, swirling the pan occasionally, until it is nut brown in color. Reduce the heat to simmer and stir in the parsley, Parmesan, Italian seasoning, oregano, capers, garlic, and yogurt, stirring until the mixture is well combined.

Add the beans, peas, salt, and pepper and continue to cook, stirring gently, for 2 minutes or until the beans and peas are heated through and completely coated with the sauce. Serve immediately.

- ³/₄ stick (6 tablespoons) unsalted butter
- ¹/₄ cup minced fresh parsley leaves
- ¹/₄ cup freshly grated Parmesan cheese
- ¹/₂ teaspoon Italian seasoning, crumbled
- ¹/₄ teaspoon dried oregano, crumbled
- 2 tablespoons drained bottled capers or more to taste
- 1 teaspoon minced garlic
- ¹/₂ cup low-fat or nonfat plain yogurt
- 2 15-ounce cans white beans, drained and rinsed
- 1 10-ounce package frozen tiny peas (petits pois), thawed
- ¹/₂ teaspoon salt or to taste
- ¹/₂ teaspoon freshly ground pepper or more to taste

White Beans with Garlic-Cilantro Salsa

This is such a simple dish to prepare yet so flavorful, piquant, and satisfying that we make it often for family meals. Here we use cilantro as the herb, but we've also made it with fresh basil and changed the ethnicity of the dish instantly from Mexican to Italian. We like to serve it at room temperature to preserve all the fresh flavors. During tomato season, use four large red vine-ripened tomatoes instead of the canned.

1 35-ounce can Italian plum tomatoes, drained and coarsely chopped

1 tablespoon minced garlic

3/4 cup firmly packed chopped cilantro leaves

1 teaspoon salt or to taste

1/2 teaspoon freshly ground pepper, or more to taste

1 jalapeño chili, seeded, deveined (wear rubber gloves), and finely chopped

1/4 cup olive oil

2 15-ounce cans cannellini, drained and rinsed

1/2 cup grated Monterey Jack or Parmesan cheese if desired

In a glass or ceramic serving bowl, combine everything but the beans and cheese. Toss well to combine. This can be done up to 2 or 3 hours ahead, covered, and allowed to mellow at room temperature.

Just before serving, fold in the drained and rinsed beans. Pass the cheese at the table if you like.

White Beans with Orecchiette, Tomatoes, and Broccoli Rabe

SERVES 4

Orecchiette are rounds of thin, slightly bumpy pasta. The name translates as "little ears," although they resemble no ears we've ever seen. Be that as it may, they are delicious, especially when paired with broccoli rabe, the bitter-edged Italian broccoli that is mostly leaves and stems with a few slim florets thrown in just for identification purposes. Neither is always easy to find, but both are well worth searching out at an Italian salumeria or farmer's market during the season. Thanks to the alchemy created by these two ingredients and white beans, we think you'll find this a friendly, happy dish with distinct yet completely compatible flavors and textures.

Cut or break off the tough part of the stems from broccoli rabe, separate the florets, and tear the large leaves into small, manageable pieces.

In a large skillet or sauté pan over moderately high heat, bring the oil to rippling. Add the garlic, red pepper flakes, and Italian seasoning and cook until the garlic barely turns golden, about 1 minute. Add the broccoli rabe and cook, stirring, until wilted, about 2 minutes. Stir in the beans, tomatoes, salt, and pepper and simmer, stirring occasionally, for 5 minutes.

Meanwhile, in a kettle of boiling salted water, cook the orecchiette until al dente, about 8 minutes. Drain in a colander and transfer to the skillet when the vegetables are finished cooking. Toss the orecchiette with the broccoli rabe/bean mixture and the cheese.

Serve immediately, passing more grated cheese at the table if desired.

1 1/2 pounds broccoli rabe

1/3 cup olive oil

1 tablespoon minced garlic

1/2 teaspoon hot red pepper flakes

1/2 teaspoon Italian seasoning, crumbled

1 15-ounce can small white beans, drained and rinsed

1 28-ounce can Italian plum tomatoes, cut into bite-size pieces, with their juice

1/2 teaspoon salt or to taste

1/2 teaspoon freshly ground black pepper

1 pound orecchiette or small pasta shells

1/4 cup grated Pecorino Romano or Parmesan cheese, plus more for serving if desired

Yellow White Beans
with Artichokes, Capers, and Tomatoes

SERVES 6

One night while eating saffron rice at a Spanish restaurant in the neighborhood, we wondered why we couldn't turn white beans the same sunny yellow color, making them even more attractive. We knew that color adds so much to the perception of taste and the enjoyment of food, and yellow beans could look especially handsome with a red and/or green sauce—adding an unexpected visual dimension to a dish. Saffron is much too expensive to experiment with, so we used "the poor man's saffron," turmeric. It worked wonderfully well, and turmeric has been our coloring agent ever since.

FOR THE SAUCE

2 tablespoons olive oil

1 teaspoon dried oregano, crumbled

1 tablespoon minced fresh basil leaves or 1 teaspoon dried, crumbled

½ teaspoon ground coriander

1 medium onion, chopped

2 tablespoons minced garlic

1 28-ounce can Italian plum tomatoes, chopped, with their juice

1 6-ounce jar marinated artichoke hearts, drained and quartered

3 tablespoons drained bottled capers

salt and freshly ground pepper to taste

¼ cup minced fresh parsley leaves

To make the sauce, in a sauté pan over moderate heat, bring the oil to rippling. Add the oregano, basil, and coriander and stir for 30 seconds, until fragrant. Add the onion and garlic and sauté, stirring, until the onion is softened and the garlic has just turned golden. Stir in the tomatoes with their juice and simmer the mixture for 5 minutes. Stir in the artichokes and capers and cook for 2 minutes more. Season with salt and pepper, add the parsley, stir to combine, cover, reduce the heat to very low, and keep warm while you make the beans.

To make the beans, in a large skillet over moderate heat, bring the oil to rippling. Add the garlic and sauté until it just turns golden, about 1 minute. Add the turmeric and beans, stirring, for 2 minutes or until heated through. Add the broth, salt, and pepper and simmer for 2 or 3 minutes, stirring occasionally, or until the liquid is practically absorbed.

To serve, mound the beans on a warm serving platter and spoon the sauce over the beans.

Serve immediately, passing the Parmesan at the table.

FOR THE BEANS

2 tablespoons olive oil

1 tablespoon minced garlic

$^1/_2$ teaspoon ground turmeric

2 15-ounce cans white beans, drained and rinsed

$^1/_4$ cup chicken broth or water

salt and freshly ground pepper to taste

freshly grated Parmesan cheese for serving

WRAPPED
SALADS

_____

We've come up with a new, innovative way to serve a salad. It's territory occupied by ethnic foods like sushi, burritos, tacos, stuffed cabbage, crepes, and blinis—food filled with other food. We enclose chopped, well-dressed vegetables and beans in blanched, slightly crisp lettuce leaves, creating delightful little bundles of flavor and texture that can be eaten out of hand, with a knife and fork as a salad course, a first course, or side dish, or as part of an hors d'oeuvre plate.

These salads can be served naked, if you don't want to take the time to fold them into their pretty lettuce jackets. Not as much fun, of course—the surprise, the joy of discovery, is missing—but just as delicious.

METHOD FOR WRAPPING CHOPPED SALADS
IN LETTUCE LEAVES

Bring a large skillet of lightly salted water to a boil. Add two large lettuce leaves (from heads of romaine, iceberg, or Chinese, regular, or savoy cabbage) or three small leaves (from radicchio, Boston, etc.) to the pan and blanch for 30 seconds. Using tongs, transfer the lettuce to a bowl of ice water to stop the cooking. Remove the leaves from the ice water and pat dry with paper towels. Repeat with any remaining leaves.

Spread the lettuce leaves out on a work surface, rib side down, and flatten the center of each leaf with the heel of your hand, taking care not to crack or split the leaves all the way through the ribs. Place a portion of the chopped salad on the bottom half of the leaf. Bring the two sides of the leaf over the sides of the mound of salad. Fold the bottom of the leaf over the mound of salad, then fold again to wrap completely, ending with the seam side under. Transfer the salad package with a metal spatula to a serving platter or individual serving plates.

Most of our wrapped salads can also be used to fill endive leaves for fingerfood hors d'oeuvres. Place about 1 tablespoon on each leaf and decorate, if you like, with an appropriate sprig of fresh herb.

Warm Black Bean, Radish, and Scallion Salad

You can wrap this salad in lettuce leaves as we suggest or omit the leaves and serve it hot as a side dish. We happen to love the taste of sautéed radishes, and they take on another dimension when combined with black beans and scallions. The butter, unusual in a salad but perfect with the radishes, is the French tie that binds all these disparate ingredients together. The radishes stain their color and crunch.

2 tablespoons unsalted butter

4 cups (about 40) coarsely chopped radishes

4 scallions, both white and green parts, finely chopped

1 cup black beans, drained and rinsed

2 dashes of Maggi seasoning

2 tablespoons minced fresh parsley or cilantro leaves

1 teaspoon freshly grated lemon zest

salt and freshly ground pepper to taste

8 large iceberg lettuce leaves

In a skillet or sauté pan over moderate heat, melt the butter. When the foam subsides, add the radishes and scallions and cook, stirring occasionally, for about 3 minutes or until the radishes are barely tender. Add the beans and Maggi and cook, stirring gently, until the beans are just heated through, about 2 minutes more.

Remove the skillet from the heat and stir in the parsley leaves, lemon zest, salt, and pepper. Let cool for a few minutes, then divide the salad equally among the lettuce leaves, prepared as described at the beginning of the chapter. Use the method at the beginning of the chapter also for wrapping the salad. Serve warm.

Black-Eyed Pea, Tomato, and Ricotta Salata Wrapped Salad

This is a partially cooked salad in which the flavors meld subtly. If you can find ricotta salata at your cheese store or Italian salumeria and have never tasted it before, try it. It's a salted sheep's milk cheese—a hard version of the creamy ricotta you're familiar with—that's related to Greek feta but not as sharp. It's quite fresh tasting and lifts almost any salad out of the ordinary. But use feta if it's unavailable.

In a small skillet, bring the oil to rippling over moderately high heat. Add the shallots and cook until softened. Stir in the tomatoes, salt, and pepper (at least $1/2$ teaspoon or more) and cook, stirring, for 30 seconds or until just heated through. Pour off any excess liquid.

In a bowl, toss together the tomato mixture with the black-eyed peas, ricotta salata, chives, and vinegar. Taste for seasoning.

Mound about 3 tablespoons of salad on each lettuce leaf, using the method at the beginning of this chapter for preparing the lettuce leaves and wrapping the salad.

1 tablespoon olive oil

2 large shallots, thinly sliced

2 cups chopped seeded ripe tomatoes or drained canned Italian plum tomatoes

salt and freshly ground pepper to taste

1 15-ounce can black-eyed peas, drained and rinsed

2 ounces ricotta salata or feta, finely diced

$1/2$ cup minced fresh chives or scallions, both white and green parts

2 teaspoons balsamic vinegar or to taste

8 large romaine lettuce leaves

Wrapped Hummus and Vegetable Salad

Hummus lends itself perfectly to yet another of our unique wrapped salads. Here we spread it on the lettuce leaf before mounding the vegetables and enclosing it. But we have also served it another way, as part of an hors d' oeuvre plate: We mix the hummus into the vegetable mixture, spread it over each lettuce leaf, tightly roll up the leaf jelly-roll fashion, trim the ends, slice each roll crosswise with a serrated knife into about 6 pieces, and spear them with toothpicks. Two or three slices sprinkled with additional sesame seeds are a vibrant and robust addition to a colorful plate of little tastes.

8 romaine lettuce leaves

2 cups hummus (recipe
    follows)

1/2 cup chopped seeded
    cucumber

1 large carrot, grated

1 medium sweet onion, finely
    chopped

1/2 cup shredded or chopped
    radish (about 6)

1/2 cup bean sprouts

2 tablespoons chopped
    cilantro leaves

1 tablespoon toasted sesame
    seeds

salt and freshly ground
    pepper to taste

Prepare the lettuce leaves as described at the beginning of this chapter. Spread 1/4 cup of hummus on the bottom third of each leaf.

In a bowl, lightly toss together the remaining ingredients and mound an equal portion of the mixture on the hummus. Use the method at the beginning of the chapter for wrapping the salad.

Hummus bi Tahini

Spooned into a serving bowl and garnished with chopped cilantro, parsley, chopped scallions, chopped mint, or basil, hummus can be served at a buffet or with drinks surrounded by toasted pita wedges or sesame crackers. But it is especially interesting and surprising when served as an ingredient in a wrapped salad.

In a food processor, blend together all the ingredients, scraping down the sides, until the mixture is smooth. Add a tablespoon or two of water and pulse, adding more water if necessary, until the puree has a creamy texture. Taste for seasoning and add more lemon juice, garlic, pepper, cumin, or paprika.

Note: Hummus is traditionally made with chickpeas, but it can be just as delicious made with black beans, red kidney beans, pintos, or other beans that you have on hand. The texture may be slightly smoother and looser (so be sure to test for texture before adding any water), and of course the color may be different, but the flavor will remain almost the same.

$3/4$ cup tahini

1 tablespoon olive oil

$3/4$ cup fresh lemon juice or more to taste

1 tablespoon minced garlic or more to taste

$1/2$ teaspoon freshly ground pepper or more to taste

1 teaspoon ground cumin

1 19-ounce can chickpeas, drained and rinsed

$1/4$ teaspoon hot paprika or cayenne pepper or more to taste

salt to taste

Green Bean and Celeriac
Wrapped Salad in Mustard Vinaigrette

MAKES 16 SALAD PACKAGES, SERVING 8 AS A SALAD COURSE
OR APPETIZER OR 4 AS A LUNCH OR LIGHT SUPPER DISH

We like the way the French combine celeriac in a mustardy salad dressing with haricots verts, the skinny little immature green beans you can find at a price at specialty produce markets. If you don't want to spring for the high cost of the French beans, slender fresh American green beans will do very nicely.

3 tablespoons fresh lemon
  juice

2 teaspoons Dijon mustard

1 teaspoon mustard seeds,
  crushed slightly in a garlic
  press or mortar and pestle

4 dashes of Maggi seasoning

1/2 teaspoon salt or to taste

1/2 teaspoon freshly ground
  pepper

1/4 cup olive oil

1 1/4 pounds celeriac (celery
  root)

1 pound green beans or
  haricots verts, cut into
  1/2-inch pieces

2 shallots, finely chopped

16 large iceberg lettuce leaves

In a large bowl, whisk together the lemon juice, Dijon mustard, mustard seeds, Maggi, salt, and pepper and add the olive oil in a stream, whisking until the dressing is combined and emulsified.

With a sharp knife, cut off the ends of the celeriac and peel it. Rinse and dry it and cut it in half lengthwise. Cut the celeriac crosswise into 1/8-inch slices, pile up several slices at a time, and cut the slices into 1/8-inch strips. Stack the strips lengthwise and cut them into tiny dice. Add the celeriac to the dressing and toss to coat.

In a saucepan of boiling salted water, cook the green beans until crisp-tender, about 4 or 5 minutes. Drain and refresh under cold water, then drain again. Add the green beans and shallots to the celeriac mixture and toss well.

Use the method at the beginning of the chapter for preparing the lettuce leaves and wrapping the salad.

French Green Lentil, Sun-Dried Tomato, and Feta Wrapped Salad

SERVES 4

Lentilles Le Puy are from a region in south-central France and are smaller and rounder and hold their shape better than our supermarket lentils. The texture of these lentils is finer and the taste a little on the peppery side, which makes them perfect for a salad like this one. You can find lentilles Le Puy at specialty food shops and some supermarkets. Use the American variety if French lentils are not available. We like the sharpness of Greek feta cheese with French lentils, but you can substitute the milder Italian ricotta salata (a solid form of the soft ricotta you're familiar with).

In a large saucepan over high heat, bring the lentils to a boil with water to cover, reduce the heat to simmer, and cook for about 20 minutes or until just tender. Drain the lentils in a sieve and rinse with cool water.

In a large bowl, whisk together the oil, vinegar, Maggi, thyme, sun-dried tomatoes, onion, salt, and pepper. Add the lentils and toss well. Gently fold in the feta.

Use the method at the beginning of this chapter for preparing the lettuce leaves and wrapping the salad. Serve on individual salad plates.

As you spoon the salad onto the leaves, tip the spoon against the side of the bowl to drain some of the dressing from the lentils. We like this dressing, but it should just coat the ingredients, not run down your sleeve.

1 cup *lentilles Le Puy* or regular lentils

3 tablespoons extra-virgin olive oil

2 tablespoons white wine vinegar

4 dashes of Maggi seasoning

1/4 teaspoon dried thyme, crumbled

1/4 cup drained finely chopped oil-packed sun-dried tomatoes

1 small red onion, finely chopped

salt and freshly ground pepper to taste

2 ounces feta cheese, crumbled (about 1/2 cup)

4 large iceberg lettuce leaves

Salad of Petits Pois, Arugula, and Ricotta Salata

MAKES 8 SALAD PACKAGES, SERVING 4 AS A LUNCH OR LIGHT SUPPER DISH OR 8 AS A FIRST COURSE OR SIDE DISH

Sometimes our salad ingredients are determined partially by a salad's color scheme. For this one, green on green spotted with white: the bright, intense green of the tiny peas against the deep, dark forest green of the arugula. In between are little polka dots of white ricotta salata or feta. The flavors follow through: the bland sweetness of the peas contrasts with the tanginess of the arugula and the spirited freshness and saltiness of the ricotta salata. Unlike most salads, the greens in this one are cooked, then cooled. If arugula is not available, the salad works almost as well with spinach or escarole.

2 bunches of arugula (about 1¼ pounds)

2 tablespoons olive oil

6 large garlic cloves, minced and mashed to a paste with salt to taste

½ teaspoon freshly ground pepper or more to taste

1½ cups frozen tiny peas (petits pois), thawed

½ cup crumbled ricotta salata (about 2½ ounces)

8 large iceberg lettuce leaves

Remove and discard any coarse stems from the arugula. Float the leaves in a large bowl of water, agitating the greens lightly to let the sand and dirt fall to the bottom of the bowl. Remove the arugula from the water, pat dry with paper towels, and finely chop.

In a large skillet over moderately high heat, bring the oil to rippling and in it cook the garlic paste, stirring, for 1 minute. Add the arugula and pepper and sauté, stirring, until wilted and tender, about 2 minutes. Pour off any excess liquid and transfer the arugula to a bowl to cool in the refrigerator for about 10 minutes.

Lightly stir the peas and ricotta salata into the cooled arugula and mound 2 or 3 tablespoons of the mixture on each lettuce leaf, prepared as described at the beginning of this chapter.

Use the method at the beginning of the chapter for preparing the lettuce leaves and wrapping the salad.

Red Bean Cobb Salad

MAKES 8 SALAD PACKAGES. SERVING 4 AS A LUNCH OR LIGHT SUPPER
DISH OR 8 AS A FIRST COURSE OR SALAD COURSE

The original recipe for Cobb salad was invented decades ago in Hollywood. It had cheddar cheese among the ingredients and Roquefort sprinkled on top. Cobb salad has endured despite the glut of cheese. In our version the cheddar cheese is left out and beans are added for a glut of nutrition instead. We also decided to wrap it in a turban of lettuce for a more glamorous presentation as befits its origin.

1 teaspoon Dijon mustard

1 tablespoon red wine vinegar

salt and freshly ground pepper
   to taste

4 dashes of Maggi seasoning or more
   to taste

3 tablespoons olive oil

1 small ripe avocado, peeled, pitted,
   and finely chopped

2 cups finely diced cooked chicken
   (about 1 whole breast)

1/2 cup finely chopped watercress

1/2 cup finely chopped scallions, both
   white and green parts

1/2 cup finely chopped peeled and
   seeded ripe tomato

4 slices bacon, cooked crisp and
   crumbled

1/2 cup crumbled Roquefort cheese
   (about 2 ounces)

1 cup drained and rinsed canned red
   beans

1 hard-cooked egg, sieved

8 large romaine lettuce leaves

In a bowl, whisk together the mustard, vinegar, salt, pepper, and Maggi. Add the oil in a stream, whisking briskly until the dressing is emulsified.

Add the remaining ingredients except the lettuce leaves to the dressing and toss lightly to coat.

Use the method at the beginning of this chapter for preparing the lettuce leaves and wrapping the salad.

White Beans and Herbed Shrimp with Watercress

This salad can be made with almost any kind or color of bean. We've chosen white because shrimp are white when cooked and mayonnaise is sort of white. The result is an off-white mixture flecked with the deep green of watercress. Cutting open or biting into the lettuce package reveals a cooling color scheme. But you can use black beans for a chiaroscuro effect, red beans for a pink and rosy look, and so on. You can even change the color of the package by using red cabbage leaves instead of romaine.

1¼ **pounds small shrimp (about 60), peeled and deveined**

1 15-ounce **can small white cannellini or navy beans**

½ **cup homemade or good-quality bottled mayonnaise**

½ **cup finely diced celery**

3 or 4 **scallions, both white and green parts, thinly sliced**

2 **tablespoons minced fresh dill**

1 **tablespoon fresh lemon juice**

1 **tablespoon Dijon mustard**

1 **cup finely chopped watercress**

½ **teaspoon salt or to taste**

½ **teaspoon freshly ground white pepper or to taste**

8 **large romaine lettuce leaves**

In a large saucepan of salted boiling water, cook the shrimp for 1 minute or until just cooked through. Drain in a colander and cool for 5 minutes, then run under cold water to cool completely. Coarsely chop the shrimp and in a bowl toss lightly with the remaining ingredients except the lettuce leaves.

Use the method at the beginning of the chapter for preparing the lettuce leaves and wrapping the salad.

SALADS
BIG AND
SMALL

Curried Adzuki Bean, Chicken, and Tomato Salad

SERVES 4

Adzuki beans are little red beans that look as if they were designed by some Japanese national treasure. The dried bean is a dusty maroon color with a black and white keel. They look beautiful piled in a glass jar on a kitchen shelf, and they taste just as good. Adzukis are the beans in red bean ice cream. They are often served as a sweet in Japan and are the perfect bean for a curried salad like this one. Until recently we hadn't seen them in cans, but now some enlightened manufacturer has understood their increasing popularity. The cans we found are distributed by Eden Foods and are on the shelves of some specialty food shops and most health food stores. They're made from organically grown beans and very low in sodium.

2 tablespoons canola or peanut oil

1 large garlic clove, minced

2 whole skinless, boneless chicken breasts, cut into bite-size pieces

1 medium yellow onion, chopped

1 cup tomato sauce

1/4 cup minced cilantro leaves

2 tablespoons garam masala or curry powder

1/4 teaspoon cayenne pepper

1 tablespoon red wine vinegar

1 15-ounce can adzuki beans, drained and rinsed

salt and freshly ground black pepper to taste

1/2 cup low-fat or nonfat plain yogurt or more to taste

2 tablespoons slivered or sliced almonds, lightly toasted

1/2 cup thinly sliced scallions, both white and green parts

In a large skillet or sauté pan over moderate heat, bring the oil to rippling and in it cook the garlic, stirring, for 1 minute. Add the chicken pieces and stir until the chicken has browned slightly and is cooked through, about 2 or 3 minutes more. Remove the chicken with a slotted spoon and set aside in a serving bowl.

In the oil remaining in the pan, sauté the onion until softened and pale golden, about 5 minutes. Add the tomato sauce, cilantro, garam masala, cayenne, vinegar, adzuki beans, salt, and pepper. Simmer the sauce for 2 minutes and add it to the chicken. Stir in the yogurt and toss the salad well.

Let it cool to room temperature and serve sprinkled with the almonds and scallions.

Note: Steamed or boiled basmati rice, cooled, makes a nice accompaniment.

Black Bean and Orzo Salad
with Turkey and Bell Peppers

SERVES 6

Leftover turkey is often a postholiday problem. What do you do with it that's not a cliché? A salad like this one is a perfect answer. The dressing is zippy and a little hot, the ingredients as colorful as a handful of confetti. The finished product is so good we often make it from scratch, roasting or poaching half a breast just for this recipe. Using the cooked remains of a holiday bird, though, qualifies this as fast food. Cooking the orzo, chopping the vegetables and herbs, blending the dressing, and tossing the salad brings it to the table in only about 15 to 20 minutes.

½ pound orzo (about 1¼ cups)

3 tablespoons fresh lime juice

1½ tablespoons white wine vinegar

2 large garlic cloves, chopped

2 fresh or pickled jalapeño chilies, seeded, deveined (wear rubber gloves), and chopped

1½ teaspoons ground cumin or more to taste

½ teaspoon salt or to taste

1 teaspoon freshly ground pepper

½ teaspoon dry mustard

1 teaspoon Maggi seasoning

⅔ cup olive oil

4 cups cooked turkey, preferably white meat, or 1 roasted or poached turkey breast half, cut into bite-size pieces

1 red bell pepper, seeded, deveined, and cut into tiny dice

1 yellow bell pepper, seeded, deveined, and cut into tiny dice

1 medium sweet red onion, chopped (about 1½ cups)

2 15-ounce cans black beans, drained and rinsed

½ cup finely chopped cilantro leaves

6 cups shredded romaine lettuce leaves if desired

In a large saucepan over moderately high heat, bring salted water to a boil. Drop in the orzo and cook for 6 to 8 minutes or until it is al dente. Drain it in a colander and rinse it under cold water, then drain again.

Meanwhile, in a food processor or blender, process the lime juice, vinegar, garlic, chilies, cumin, salt, pepper, dry mustard, and Maggi until the mixture is smooth. With the motor running, add the oil in a slow stream and continue processing until the dressing is combined and emulsified.

Transfer the drained orzo to a salad bowl and mix in the turkey, red and yellow bell peppers, onion, beans, and cilantro.

Toss the turkey/bean mixture with the dressing until coated well. Make a nest of the shredded lettuce leaves on each of 6 plates and top each nest with portions of the salad.

Crisped Black Beans with Orzo and Toasted Walnuts

Sautéing black beans makes them slightly crispy on the outside, soft and melting on the inside—the perfect foil for tiny rice-shaped orzo, cooked al dente so it's soft on the outside but still firm inside. Chili powder lends a surprising heat to this room-temperature side dish, and the walnuts contribute an elegant, elusive flavor. Try it for a special buffet served alongside other more substantial salads such as seafood, beef, or chicken. Or serve it as a first course nestled on a lettuce leaf or piled into scooped-out tomato halves (if you do, use the scallions as garnish instead of stirring them in).

2 tablespoons peanut oil

1 teaspoon chili powder

$1/2$ teaspoon salt or to taste

1 19-ounce can black beans, drained, rinsed, and patted dry with paper towels

$1/2$ pound orzo (about $1^{1}/_{4}$ cups)

1 tablespoon walnut oil (available at specialty food shops)

2 tablespoons fresh lemon juice

3 scallions, both white and green parts, finely chopped

$1/2$ cup walnut pieces, toasted

In a large skillet or sauté pan over moderately high heat, bring the peanut oil to rippling. Stir in the chili powder and salt and in the seasoned oil sauté the black beans, shaking the skillet often, until the beans are crisped, about 7 to 10 minutes. Transfer to a serving bowl.

Meanwhile, in a saucepan of boiling salted water, cook the orzo until al dente, about 6 to 8 minutes. Rinse the orzo under cold water and drain well.

In a medium bowl, toss the orzo with the walnut oil and lemon juice and add to the black beans, tossing lightly to combine. Taste for seasoning and add more salt if desired. Just before serving, stir in the scallions and the walnuts. Serve at room temperature.

Black Bean and Potato Salad with Smoked Salmon and Dill

What could be prettier or more colorful than a salad like this one? Serve it as a first course or as part of a buffet. It's easy to put together—only the potatoes need cooking, and even they take only 8 to 10 minutes. We have made this salad with smoked trout, smoked mussels, smoked oysters, or smoked turkey replacing the smoked salmon. Grated or julienned smoked cheese is also fine for a vegetarian version.

In a steamer set over boiling water, steam the potatoes, covered, for 10 minutes or until tender. Drain.

Meanwhile, in a small bowl, whisk together the vermouth, shallots, vinegar, lemon juice, and Maggi seasoning.

Transfer the still-hot potatoes to a serving bowl and toss them with the beans and the vermouth dressing. Let the salad cool for 10 minutes to almost room temperature and stir in the remaining ingredients. Toss gently to combine. Serve at room temperature or slightly chilled.

1 pound tiny new red Bliss potatoes, scrubbed and quartered

$1/3$ cup dry vermouth

2 large shallots, minced

2 tablespoons white wine vinegar

2 tablespoons fresh lemon juice

4 dashes of Maggi seasoning

1 15-ounce can black beans, drained and rinsed

$1/4$ cup olive oil

$1/4$ pound sliced smoked salmon, cut into tiny pieces

2 tablespoons minced fresh dill

2 tablespoons thinly sliced scallion greens

2 tablespoons minced fresh parsley

1 tablespoon drained bottled capers

salt and freshly ground pepper to taste

Black Bean and Turkey Salad with Honey Mustard Dressing

SERVES 8

A few years ago we reluctantly bought a fresh turkey breast at our local supermarket at the urging of a friend. We thought that we'd end up with a dry, tasteless disaster, but amazingly, it turned out to be moister and even more flavorful than the breast of a whole roast turkey we had served at a holiday meal. We still had lots left over, however, so we made this salad and took it along for a picnic after a morning of apple picking in upstate New York. It's been part of our repertoire ever since.

2 15-ounce cans black beans, drained and rinsed

1 large red onion, chopped

4 scallions, both white and green parts, chopped

4 medium red ripe tomatoes, peeled, seeded, and chopped

1 red bell pepper, seeded, deveined, and chopped

1 yellow bell pepper, seeded, deveined, and chopped

4 cups diced roast turkey breast

1 11-ounce can Green Giant corn niblets, drained well

$^1/_4$ cup red wine vinegar

$^1/_4$ cup Dijon mustard

1 teaspoon dry mustard

2 tablespoons honey

1 tablespoon minced garlic

1 teaspoon dried thyme, crushed

$^1/_4$ teaspoon cayenne pepper or more to taste

1 teaspoon salt or to taste

1 teaspoon freshly ground black pepper

1 tablespoon Maggi seasoning

$^3/_4$ cup olive oil

$^1/_2$ cup chopped cilantro leaves

In a large bowl, combine the beans, red onion, scallions, tomatoes, red and yellow bell peppers, turkey, and corn.

In a smaller bowl, whisk together the vinegar, mustards, honey, garlic, thyme, cayenne, salt, pepper, and Maggi. Add the oil in a stream, whisking, and whisk until the dressing is emulsified. (Or place the dressing ingredients in a food processor and with the motor running add the oil in a stream, processing until the dressing is emulsified.) The dressing can be made up to 1 week in advance and refrigerated.

Pour the dressing over the salad mixture, add the chopped cilantro, and toss gently until well combined.

Black-Eyed Pea, Cucumber, and Cabbage Slaw

The perfect plate-mate for a baked ham is this southern-style slaw, a fine recipe for entertaining because it can be doubled or tripled in direct proportion. It's chopped fine in the California style so it can also be bundled into blanched cabbage leaves (see preceding chapter) for a neat wrapped salad. We like to serve this savory variation on mayonnaise-dressed coleslaw with corn bread to continue the Southern theme.

In a large bowl, whisk together the vinegar, mustard, horseradish, Maggi seasoning, salt, and pepper. Add the oil in a stream, whisking until the dressing is combined and emulsified.

Add the remaining ingredients to the dressing and toss until all the vegetables are coated. Taste and add more salt and pepper if necessary.

2 tablespoons white wine vinegar

2 tablespoons Dijon mustard

2 tablespoons drained bottled horseradish

4 dashes of Maggi seasoning

salt and freshly ground pepper to taste

6 tablespoons olive or vegetable oil

2 15-ounce cans black-eyed peas, drained and rinsed

2 pounds cabbage, coarsely grated in a food processor

2 cucumbers (preferably Kirby), coarsely grated in a food processor

2 medium carrots, coarsely grated in a food processor

2 scallions, both white and green parts, minced

2 large garlic cloves, minced

2 tablespoons minced parsley

Black-Eyed Pea, Fennel, and Watercress Salad with Orange Dressing

A good salad depends on finesse and balance. Here the forceful flavors of watercress and fennel combine beautifully with the delicate taste and texture of the peas and the sassy tang of the dressing. We usually dislike the pretension of a composed salad, but this one gains with a little mound building: a bed of watercress with slim crescents of fennel nestled on top and a small avalanche of black-eyed peas spilling over all. It takes a little extra effort to divide up the dressing in thirds to dress each component separately, then to assemble them on four salad plates, but it's worth it.

1 tablespoon freshly grated orange zest

2 tablespoons fresh orange juice

salt and freshly ground pepper to taste

$1/4$ cup olive oil

4 cups watercress, coarse stems removed

1 fennel bulb (about $3/4$ to 1 pound), thinly sliced lengthwise

1 15-ounce can black-eyed peas, drained and rinsed

In a small bowl, whisk the orange zest and juice with salt and pepper, add the oil in a slow stream, whisking, and keep whisking until the dressing is emulsified.

In another bowl, toss the watercress with a third of the dressing until it is coated well and divide it among 4 salad plates.

In the same bowl, toss the fennel with half the remaining dressing until it is coated well and mound it in equal portions in the center of the watercress.

Again in the same bowl, toss the peas with the remaining dressing until all the peas are coated well and spoon them equally over the fennel.

Chickpeas with Beet Greens, Onion, and Garlic

SERVES 4

What do you do with beet tops? Well, whatever you do, don't throw them out—and don't leave them in the greengrocer's trash bin unless they're wilted. Cut them about 1¹/₂ inches from the roots, break off the tough part of their stems, wash them, pat them dry with paper towels, and store them in a plastic bag in the refrigerator. They'll last for a few days until you decide to make this wonderfully delicate dish and serve it cold or at room temperature with other salads at a buffet or as a side dish with fish or chicken breasts or as a first course. You can also try this with Swiss Chard (actually a sibling of beet greens; it is beets cultivated for the leaves rather than the roots), spinach, broccoli rabe, or radicchio. Don't substitute other beans for the chickpeas, though, because this dish needs that subtle chickpea crunch.

In a large skillet or sauté pan over moderate heat, bring the oil to rippling, add the onion and garlic, and sauté until the onion is softened but not colored, about 5 minutes.

Add the chickpeas and tomatoes and cook, stirring often, for 5 minutes. Stir in the beet greens, turn the heat down to simmer, cover, and cook until the greens are just wilted, about 2 minutes.

Remove the skillet from the heat and stir in the lemon juice, salt, and pepper. Allow to cool to room temperature before serving.

2 tablespoons light olive oil

1 medium onion, halved and thinly sliced

1 large garlic clove, thinly sliced

1 15-ounce can chickpeas, drained and rinsed

1¹/₂ cups canned Italian tomatoes with some of their juice

1 pound beet greens (if you have more, use them— exact measurements aren't important), coarsely chopped

juice of ¹/₂ lemon

salt and freshly ground pepper to taste

Cicero Salad with Mustard Bread Crumbs

SERVES 4

This could have been called a Caesar salad. But because we have added nourishing, starchy chickpeas and Cicero's family name stemmed from the Italian word for chickpeas (ceci), it seemed right to call it a Cicero salad. In Italy chickpeas are grown mostly in the South but are popular all over the country as they are everywhere in the Mediterranean, especially in the Middle East, where they have been cultivated for thousands of years. Chickpeas, along with lentils and fava beans, were the only beans Europeans knew before 1492 and the introduction of New World agricultural products like kidney beans and other future food stars destined to cause a revolution in the European kitchen—tomatoes, potatoes, chilies, vanilla, and chocolate.

FOR THE MUSTARD BREAD CRUMBS

$^1/_2$ stick ($^1/_4$ cup) unsalted butter

1 large garlic clove, crushed in a garlic press

1 tablespoon finely chopped fresh parsley

$1^1/_2$ tablespoons Dijon mustard

2 cups fresh bread crumbs

FOR THE DRESSING

2 large garlic cloves, chopped

2 tablespoons fresh lemon juice

2 tablespoons good-quality bottled mayonnaise

$^1/_4$ teaspoon salt

$^1/_2$ teaspoon freshly ground pepper

1 tablespoon Maggi seasoning

$^1/_3$ cup olive oil

2 tablespoons water

FOR THE SALAD

1 15-ounce can chickpeas, drained and rinsed

1 head romaine lettuce, trimmed and torn into bite-size pieces

$^1/_3$ cup freshly grated Parmesan cheese

12 pimiento-stuffed green olives, sliced

1 2-ounce can flat anchovies, drained, patted dry, and cut in half

Make the bread crumbs: In a small saucepan over moderate heat, melt the butter. When the foam subsides, add the garlic and parsley and cook for 1 minute. Stir in the mustard until well combined, then add the bread crumbs and toss with a fork until coated with the mustard/butter mixture and separated. If made ahead, keep warm in a 200° oven until ready to use.

Make the dressing: In a blender or food processor, blend together the garlic, lemon juice, mayonnaise, salt, pepper, and Maggi seasoning until smooth. With the motor running, add the oil in a slow stream and blend until combined and emulsified. Add the water and blend the dressing well.

Make the salad: In a large salad bowl, toss the chickpeas and romaine with the dressing until well coated. Add the Parmesan, olives, anchovies, and mustard bread crumbs and toss again to combine.

Note: We think you'll find many uses for mustard bread crumbs. They're wonderful as a topping for cooked vegetables like cauliflower, broccoli, green beans, asparagus, zucchini, or brussels sprouts.

Sprinkle them on other salads; over seafood and gratins; bread veal chops, fish fillets, and pork medallions with them.

Best of all, add their flavor and crunch to other beans that have been simply heated in a little water or broth, drained, and combined with the bread crumbs; they'll require no other seasoning.

Chickpea, Mussel, and Salmon Salad with Kalamata Olives

SERVES 6 TO 8

What to bring to a picnic or a lawn concert in the park? We found cans of salmon and mussels on our kitchen shelf one day and whipped up this main-dish salad as our contribution to an elegant blanket dinner before listening to the 1812 Overture under the stars. The salad is substantial yet light, and it doesn't need the cliché accompaniments of potato salad and coleslaw to round it out. Canned mussels, we've discovered, are great to have on hand for just such an improvisation. They're so fresh and clean tasting that you can use them without shame to replace clams in a garlicky red or white sauce for pasta or napped with rémoulade *for a first course. Believe us, no one will suspect that you didn't cook them in the shell.*

1 15-ounce can salmon, drained and flaked, the juice reserved

1 15-ounce can mussels in water, drained

2 tablespoons fresh lemon juice

1 15-ounce can small chickpeas, drained and rinsed

2 large red bell peppers, seeded, deveined, and cut into $^1/_2$-inch dice

$2^1/_2$ cups thinly sliced celery

1 large red onion, chopped (about $1^1/_4$ cups or more)

$1^1/_4$ cups Kalamata or other oil- or brine-cured black olives, pitted and thinly sliced

$^1/_4$ cup minced fresh dill

3 tablespoons white wine vinegar

3 tablespoons homemade or good-quality bottled mayonnaise

2 tablespoons Dijon mustard

salt and freshly ground pepper to taste

$^1/_2$ cup olive oil

In a large bowl, toss together the salmon, mussels, lemon juice, chickpeas, bell peppers, celery, onion, olives, and dill.

In a small bowl, whisk the reserved salmon juice with the vinegar, mayonnaise, mustard, salt, and pepper. Add the oil in a stream, whisking briskly until the mixture is emulsified.

Add the dressing to the salad and toss the salad well. Taste for seasoning and add more salt and pepper if necessary.

Tunisian-Style Glazed Chickpea and Carrot Salad

SERVES 6

Jellel Gasteli, a Tunisian photographer who now lives in Paris with his wife, Sally's cousin Dorine, informed us that all Tunisians love sweets, and perhaps that's why carrots are so popular there. This salad combines the sweetness of carrots with a special combination of Tunisian and Moroccan spices along with raisins. It is usually made with cooked carrots alone but sometimes with artichokes as well, Jellel told us. The chickpeas are our variation. They're used often in Tunisian cooking.

In a saucepan over high heat, bring the carrots and water to cover to a boil, reduce the heat to simmer, and cook the carrots for 5 minutes or until barely tender. Drain the carrots and set aside, reserving $1/2$ cup of the cooking liquid.

In a skillet over moderate heat, bring the oil to rippling. Add the onions and cook for about 10 minutes or until they are soft and golden. Add the raisins, the reserved carrot cooking liquid, the red pepper flakes, caraway seeds, paprika, cumin, and salt, increase the heat to moderately high, bring the liquid to a boil, and add the reserved carrots. Reduce the heat to simmer and cook the carrots, uncovered, for about 5 minutes or until the liquid is reduced slightly.

Stir in the chickpeas and cayenne and continue to stir until the chickpeas are heated through, about 2 minutes, and the vegetables are coated with the glaze.

Serve the salad warm or at room temperature, squeezing the lemon juice over it just before serving.

$1^1/2$ **pounds carrots, scraped, quartered lengthwise, and sliced $1/8$ inch thick**

3 tablespoons canola or peanut oil

2 onions, halved lengthwise and thinly sliced crosswise

2 tablespoons golden raisins, plumped in hot water for 10 minutes

$1/2$ teaspoon hot red pepper flakes

$1/2$ teaspoon caraway seeds

$1/2$ teaspoon sweet paprika

$1/2$ teaspoon ground cumin

$1/2$ teaspoon salt

1 15-ounce can chickpeas, drained and rinsed

cayenne or freshly ground pepper to taste

juice of 1 lemon

Fava Bean, Orange, and Knockwurst Salad

SERVES 6

A main-dish salad is good any time of the year, but one as hearty and robust as this one deserves to be served during the cold months (perhaps following a bowl of hot soup), when oranges are plentiful and salads seem to be an anachronism. It's a seemingly discordant blend of ingredients—garlicky sausages with oranges, sage, onion, fava beans, and bitter greens—but it works. All you need to add is a loaf of French bread or pumpernickel, and you'll have some very satisfied diners sitting around your table.

1 pound all-beef knockwurst

¹/₄ cup dry white wine

¹/₄ cup white wine vinegar

1 tablespoon Dijon mustard

¹/₄ cup chopped fresh sage leaves

6 dashes of Maggi seasoning or more to taste

salt and freshly ground pepper to taste

¹/₃ cup olive oil

1 15-ounce can fava beans, drained and rinsed

1 large red onion, cut in half and thinly sliced

2 celery ribs, thinly sliced

1 large navel orange, peeled, cut into segments, membranes and pith discarded, and segments cut into bite-size pieces

6 cups assorted greens such as arugula, watercress, Belgian endive, frisée (curly endive), spinach, and escarole, torn into bite-size pieces

In a saucepan over moderately high heat, combine the knockwurst with cold water, bring to a boil, and cook for 10 minutes or until plumped. Drain, let cool slightly, and cut diagonally into ³/₈-inch slices.

Meanwhile, in a small bowl, whisk together the white wine, vinegar, mustard, sage, Maggi, salt, and pepper. Whisk in the oil in a slow stream, whisking until the mixture is emulsified.

In a large bowl, toss the beans, onion, celery, and orange with about two thirds of the dressing.

In another bowl, toss the greens with the remaining dressing.

Divide the greens among 4 dinner plates. Mound an equal portion of the bean mixture on the center of the greens and equal portions of the knockwurst slices over the bean mixture. (The knockwurst slices can be added when still warm or at room temperature.)

Note: If you can't find fava beans, chickpeas, frozen limas (10-ounce package), pigeon peas, or other firm-textured large beans make adequate substitutes.

Fava Bean Succotash Salad
with Scallops and Mexican Spices

Talk about fusion cooking! This recipe combines a little bit of Italy, New England, Mexico, the Southwest, and India. We'll let you decide which ingredients and techniques come from where—your mouth won't care. This is such an easy way to cook— it's almost not *cooking (just the cumin seeds hit the pan). We use raw scallops marinated briefly in lime juice to make this dish more interesting, substantial, and very fresh tasting by combining them with the succotash duo, beans and corn. You can use parsley instead of the cilantro called for and a yellow pepper instead of red (but not green). This is a well-seasoned salad that needs no accompaniment except a lettuce leaf on which to serve it add a coarse textured bread and there's dinner.*

$^{1}/_{2}$ teaspoon cumin seeds

1$^{1}/_{2}$ pounds bay scallops

2 teaspoons freshly grated lime zest

$^{1}/_{2}$ cup fresh lime juice

2 tablespoons vegetable oil

2 large garlic cloves, minced

2 fresh jalapeño chilies, seeded, deveined (wear rubber gloves), and minced

1 red bell pepper, seeded, deveined, and cut into tiny dice

1 celery rib, cut into tiny dice

1 cup thinly sliced sweet red onion (or Bermuda, Maui, Walla Walla, Vidalia, or Texas Sweet)

1 11-ounce can Green Giant corn niblets, drained well

1 15-ounce can fava beans, drained and rinsed

$^{1}/_{2}$ cup minced cilantro leaves

salt and freshly ground pepper to taste

In a small dry skillet over moderate heat, toast the cumin seeds, shaking the skillet to turn the seeds, for 1 to 2 minutes or until fragrant. Cool slightly and crush the seeds in a mortar and pestle.

In a large glass or ceramic bowl, combine the scallops, lime zest, and lime juice and marinate for 10 minutes, stirring the scallops occasionally.

Stir the remaining ingredients into the scallops and toss well. Chill the salad for 15 minutes or up to 24 hours and toss again before serving.

Green Bean and Green Olive Salad

Judging from the title, you might think this salad is all green. But if you think Christmas, you have the actual color scheme well in mind. That doesn't mean that you can serve it only at the holidays. It's the kind of food that works well anytime— with drinks, served with or on thin slices of sourdough bread, as part of an antipasto plate, or as finger food wrapped in a lettuce leaf envelope (see "Wrapped Salads"). It can accompany cheese, salami, or other hors d'oeuvres, garnish grilled fish or chicken—it's really so versatile and so spirited in flavor you'll come to rely on it often.

$^1/_2$ **pound green beans, cut into $^1/_4$-inch lengths**

2 cups firmly packed drained pimiento-stuffed green olives (1 9$^1/_2$-ounce jar)

4 celery ribs, finely chopped

1 red bell pepper, seeded, deveined, and finely chopped

1 medium red onion, finely chopped

1 large garlic clove, minced and mashed to a paste with $^1/_4$ teaspoon salt

3 tablespoons minced fresh parsley leaves

1 teaspoon dried oregano, crumbled, or more to taste

$^1/_4$ **teaspoon cayenne pepper**

2 tablespoons red wine vinegar

$^1/_3$ **cup olive oil**

In a steamer or a saucepan of boiling water, cook the green beans for 2 minutes. Refresh under cold water and set aside.

Cut the olives in half lengthwise, then thinly slice them crosswise.

In a bowl, toss together everything but the vinegar and oil. Add the vinegar and oil and toss to combine the salad well.

Middle Eastern–Style Tuna Salad with Hummus

SERVES 4 TO 6

Most people think of hummus only as a dip, but it can lead another dynamic life as a dressing for salads or as a sauce for grilled fish and chicken. Here, undiluted, it is first tossed with tuna and then, thinned with a little water, drizzled over the tuna's topping of browned, almost caramelized, onions and toasted pine nuts for an unusual first course. Spoon the salad from a serving platter at the table or mound individual portions on salad plates in the kitchen. The way it's presented is part of its charm.

Heat the oil in a sauté pan over moderately high heat until it ripples. Add the onions and cook, stirring and scraping occasionally, for 20 to 25 minutes or until they are well browned. Season them with salt and pepper, transfer to a plate, and set aside.

Meanwhile, in a bowl, toss the tuna with ½ cup of the hummus until combined well. Mound the tuna mixture on a serving platter.

In the same sauté pan over moderately low heat, toast the pine nuts, stirring, until they are golden, about 3 minutes.

Sprinkle the onions and pine nuts over the tuna and drizzle the salad with the remaining hummus, thinned with a little water if it's too thick. Garnish with the chopped parsley and serve with toasted pita triangles, cocktail pumpernickel slices, or crackers.

2 tablespoons vegetable oil

1 pound yellow onions, thinly sliced (about 1½ cups)

salt and freshly ground pepper

2 6½-ounce cans solid white tuna in oil or water, drained and flaked

1 cup hummus bi tahini (page 189)

2 tablespoons pine nuts

½ cup firmly packed chopped fresh flat-leaf parsley

Curried Bean, Chicken, and Mango Chutney Salad

SERVES 4 TO 6

We have a personal aversion to cold pasta salads made with mayonnaise. They're usually glutinous and tacky when they should be silky. Beans on the other hand blend with mayonnaise most agreeably. For a fragrant, smooth, slightly sweet main-dish salad that can be served for lunch or supper nestled into crisp lettuce leaves or bedded on cooled white or basmati rice.

1 15-ounce can kidney beans, drained and rinsed

2 whole skinless, boneless chicken breasts, poached, cooled, and cut into bite-size pieces

12 cherry tomatoes, quartered

4 scallions, both white and green parts, thinly sliced

1/4 cup firmly packed finely chopped cilantro leaves

1 fresh jalapeño chili, seeded, deveined (wear rubber gloves), and minced

1 teaspoon minced garlic

1 tablespoon minced peeled fresh ginger

1/2 cup homemade or good-quality bottled mayonnaise or more to taste

1 teaspoon curry powder or more to taste

1/4 teaspoon cayenne pepper

2 tablespoons finely chopped drained mango chutney or more to taste

salt and freshly ground pepper to taste if desired

In a large bowl, combine the beans, chicken, cherry tomatoes, scallions, cilantro, and jalapeño.

In a small bowl, whisk together the garlic, ginger, mayonnaise, curry powder, cayenne, and chutney. Thin the mayonnaise mixture by whisking in about a tablespoon of water.

Add the dressing to the bean/chicken mixture, tossing until combined well. Taste for seasoning and add salt and freshly ground pepper if desired.

Garlicky Lentil Salad with Browned Sausage

SERVES 4

In this salad we fortify the garlic flavor three ways: by simmering some, sautéing some, and adding some raw at the finish. Each way adds to an arpeggio of garlic tastes.

In a saucepan over moderately high heat, combine the lentils with water to cover, the bay leaves, and 2 of the garlic cloves, smashed, and bring to a boil. Lower the heat to simmer and cook, covered, for 15 minutes. Add the salt and continue simmering for 5 minutes more or until the lentils are just tender.

Meanwhile, mince the remaining garlic and in a sauté pan or skillet over moderately high heat, bring the oil to rippling. Add about two thirds of the minced garlic, the pepper, onion, carrot, celery, and thyme and cook, stirring, for 2 minutes. Reduce the heat to moderately low and continue cooking, stirring often, for 5 minutes or until the vegetables are softened.

Drain the lentils in a sieve, discard the bay leaves, remove the garlic cloves, mash them with a fork, and add them to the vegetable mixture in the sauté pan along with the cooked lentils, vinegar, parsley, salt, pepper, and reserved minced garlic and stir the mixture to combine well. Cover and keep warm over very low heat.

In another sauté pan or skillet over moderate heat, brown the kielbasa and transfer it to paper towels to drain. Mound the lentil mixture on a serving plate or in a vegetable dish and surround it with the browned kielbasa. Serve hot, warm, or at room temperature.

2 cups lentils

2 bay leaves

6 large garlic cloves

1 teaspoon salt

2 tablespoons olive oil

$^1/_2$ teaspoon freshly ground pepper or more to taste

1 medium onion, finely chopped

1 large carrot, grated

2 celery ribs, finely chopped

1 teaspoon fresh thyme or $^1/_2$ teaspoon dried

2 tablespoons red wine vinegar or more to taste

$^1/_2$ cup minced fresh parsley leaves

$^1/_2$ pound smoked kielbasa or other ready-to-eat smoked sausage

Lentils with Blue Cheese and Bitter Greens

SERVES 4 AS A SALAD COURSE OR 6 AS A FIRST-COURSE WRAPPED
SALAD

The French love lentils as a salad. So do we. This one contrasts lentils' sweet nutty flavor with bitter greens: endive, radicchio, and arugula. You could add curly endive (frisée may be its haughty new name, but it still tastes like curly endive to us) to the mix if you like, as an addition or a substitution. Just as long as the green you add has a bitter edge, this salad will keep its character intact.

1 cup lentils

2 cups chicken broth

1 cup water

2 large garlic cloves, lightly
   mashed

1 bunch of arugula, coarse
   stems removed

1 small head of radicchio
   (about $1/2$ pound)

1 Belgian endive

3 tablespoons olive oil

1 tablespoon red wine vinegar

1 tablespoon fresh lemon
   juice

1 tablespoon Maggi seasoning

$1/2$ cup crumbled blue cheese
   (about $2^1/2$ ounces)

salt and freshly ground
   pepper to taste

In a saucepan over moderately low heat, simmer the lentils in the broth and water with the garlic, covered, for 20 minutes or until the lentils are just tender. Drain (save the cooking liquid for another use if you like), remove the garlic, and mash it with the side of a heavy knife blade.

Meanwhile, chop the arugula, radicchio, and endive into $1/4$-inch pieces.

In a salad bowl, toss the lentils with the olive oil, vinegar, lemon juice, Maggi, and mashed garlic. Add the chopped greens, blue cheese, salt, and pepper and toss well to combine. Serve slightly warm or at room temperature.

Note: To serve as a wrapped salad, blanch 6 romaine lettuce leaves and wrap the salad as described at the beginning of the "Wrapped Salads" chapter.

Succotash Salad with Lime-Cumin Vinaigrette

SERVES 4

Succotash is a popular American side dish. Toss it cooled with red bell pepper, radishes, scallions, cilantro, and a lime-cumin-flavored vinaigrette, and you can take it to the table in a completely new guise. During corn season we often roast the ears with the husks on a rack over the gas flame of our stove, which Native Americans may have done (not on the stove, of course, but in the embers of a cooking fire)—when they first combined corn and beans and named the dish—to give the salad a more toasted, earthy taste. You can substitute almost any beans for the limas—they were not cultivated by the North American tribes—and still be authentic; it's the combination of beans and corn that make it succotash. The inventive Algonquins used the corn stalks as natural bean poles, so it was natural for them to cook the two vegetables together.

In a small skillet over moderately high heat, bring 1 tablespoon of the oil to rippling. Add the corn niblets and the limas and sauté, stirring, for 3 minutes. Set aside to cool.

In a salad bowl, combine the red bell pepper, radishes, scallions, and cilantro and set aside.

In a small dry skillet over moderate heat, toast the ground cumin, stirring, until fragrant, about 1 to 2 minutes.

In a small bowl, whisk the lime juice and vinegar with the cumin, salt, and pepper. Whisk in the remaining oil in a stream and keep whisking until emulsified.

Add the corn and limas to the vegetable mixture in the salad bowl, pour the dressing over the combination, and toss. Serve cooled or at room temperature.

$^1/_4$ cup olive oil

1 15-ounce can Green Giant corn niblets, drained

1 10-ounce package frozen lima beans, thawed

1 red bell pepper, seeded, deveined, and cut into $^1/_4$-inch dice

4 red radishes, cut in half and thinly sliced

4 scallions, both white and green parts, thinly sliced

2 tablespoons chopped cilantro leaves

1 teaspoon ground cumin

$^1/_4$ cup fresh lime juice

1 tablespoon red wine vinegar

1 teaspoon salt or to taste

$^1/_4$ teaspoon freshly ground pepper or more to taste

Peas and Cauliflower in Spicy Yellow Yogurt Sauce

SERVES 4

This cool salad is slightly hot *to the tongue. It takes almost no time to prepare. All you do is break about ¹/₂ head of cauliflower into florets, boil them with the frozen peas for about 2 minutes, refresh the vegetables under cold water, and toss with the yogurt sauce. It's ready to serve then and there, or you can make it ahead and refrigerate for several hours. Either way you can use it as a side dish served with poached salmon or cold meats, as part of an hors d'oeuvre plate, or all by itself for a light lunch.*

1 small head of fresh cauliflower (1 to 1¹/₂ pounds), broken into florets

3 cups water

1 tablespoon salt or to taste

1 cup frozen tiny peas (petits pois)

2 cups low-fat plain yogurt

1 large garlic clove, finely minced

¹/₂ teaspoon ground turmeric

¹/₂ teaspoon ground cumin

¹/₂ teaspoon freshly ground black pepper

¹/₈ teaspoon cayenne pepper or more to taste

In a large pot over high heat, bring the water with 2 teaspoons of the salt to a boil, drop in the cauliflower and the peas, return to a boil, and cook for only 2 minutes. Drain in a colander and run under cold water to stop the cooking and cool. Let the vegetables drain in the colander while you prepare the dressing.

In a serving bowl, whisk together the remaining ingredients, whisking until the mixture is creamy. Fold in the vegetables gently to coat. Serve immediately or cover with plastic wrap and refrigerate for up to 4 hours, lightly tossing again before serving.

Pinto Bean, Tomato, Olive, and Tuna Salad

SERVES 4

In the late summer we make this salad with the ripest, most flavorful tomatoes we can find (we don't have to look very long or very hard: Sue's south Jersey farm stand under the blue awning at the Union Square Green Market has the best). At other times of year we use canned imported Italian plum tomatoes packed with basil (infinitely better than any out-of-season domestic or imported fresh tomatoes and much more economical). Use a sweet onion such as Maui, Vidalia, Walla Walla, or true Bermuda (not just a big yellow onion). Everything is tossed together—savory and soul satisfying!

1 1/2 tablespoons red wine vinegar

3 tablespoons olive oil or more to taste

1/2 teaspoon salt or to taste

1/2 teaspoon freshly ground pepper

1 tablespoon Maggi seasoning

1 15-ounce can pinto beans, drained and rinsed

2 pounds ripe tomatoes, seeded and chopped, or 1 28-ounce can imported Italian plum tomatoes, drained and chopped

1 1/2 cups finely chopped sweet onion

2 scallion greens, thinly sliced

1 cup large brine-cured smashed green olives with hot red pepper flakes (about 8), pitted and coarsely chopped

1/2 cup sliced fresh basil leaves

1/2 cup minced fresh parsley leaves

1 tablespoon fresh oregano leaves

1 6-ounce can solid white tuna in water, drained and flaked

In a large salad bowl, whisk together the vinegar, oil, salt, pepper, and Maggi. Stir in the beans, tomatoes, onion, scallion greens, and olives until coated well. Toss the mixture with the herbs and tuna and serve.

Note: We often serve this salad on mounds of room-temperature boiled rice or warm al dente orzo. It can also be spooned over hot spiral-shaped pasta (fusilli), in which case the recipe should serve 8 generously.

Red Bean Salad with Spinach and Walnut Dressing

Walnuts add a wonderfully surprising taste to this garlicky salad. You can try it with other beans if you feel like changing the color scheme, the taste, and/or the texture: limas, fava beans, black beans, canellini, even cooked lentils all work. Just mix gently so that the beans retain their shape and don't mash down.

1 15-ounce can red beans, drained and rinsed

$1/3$ cup light olive oil

1 10-ounce package frozen chopped spinach

$3/4$ cup walnut pieces

2 large garlic cloves, chopped

3 tablespoons red wine vinegar or 2 tablespoons balsamic vinegar

$1/4$ cup finely chopped fresh curly-leaf parsley

$1/2$ teaspoon ground coriander

$1/4$ teaspoon hot red pepper flakes

3 or 4 dashes of Maggi seasoning

juice of $1/2$ lemon or more to taste

salt and freshly ground pepper to taste

Place the beans in a salad bowl and pour the olive oil over them. Set aside.

Cook the spinach according to package directions, undercooking it slightly. Refresh under cold water, drain, and squeeze to remove any excess water.

Combine the spinach, walnuts, garlic, and vinegar in a food processor, pulsing and scraping down the sides, until the mixture is smooth.

Stir the spinach mixture gently into the beans along with the remaining ingredients. Serve at room temperature or cover tightly with plastic wrap and refrigerate for at least an hour.

If chilled, taste again for seasoning before serving.

Red Bean and Swiss Chard Cooked Salad

Cooked vegetables at room temperature are served as a salad in North Africa, where this dish originated in a slightly different guise. Ours is a little more garlicky with a hint of cinnamon just for kicks. It's delicious home cooking North African style—and proves that a salad isn't always defined by crisp, fresh greens.

Drop the Swiss chard into a kettle of boiling water set over high heat and cook it for about 10 minutes or until you can easily pierce any tough stems with a fork. Drain it well.

In a large skillet or sauté pan over moderate heat, bring the oil to rippling. Add the garlic and cook until it's golden, about 1 minute. Add the drained chard and the remaining ingredients and cook the mixture, stirring often, for 5 minutes.

Let the mixture cool and serve the salad at room temperature or refrigerate for 30 minutes and serve slightly chilled.

2 pounds Swiss chard, coarsely chopped

2 tablespoons vegetable or olive oil

2 tablespoons minced garlic

1 tablespoon hot paprika

1 tablespoon ground cumin

$1/4$ teaspoon ground cinnamon

salt and freshly ground pepper to taste

2 tablespoons fresh lemon juice

1 15-ounce can red beans, drained and rinsed

Warm Tarragon-Scented Pea Salad

SERVES 4

If you stir-fry this salad as we do here, it can be served as a side dish with a hot fall, winter, or spring meal. If the ingredients are dressed with the oil and vinegar instead of being cooked in them, it can become a first course or cool salad during any season: simply thaw the frozen peas, toss them together with the scallions, radishes, tarragon leaves, salt, and pepper, and dress the mixture with the oil and vinegar. The texture is different, the flavors less subtle, but the combination is just as welcome.

2 tablespoons olive oil

1 tablespoon white wine vinegar

1 10-ounce package frozen peas, thawed

$^{1}/_{2}$ cup finely chopped scallions, both white and green parts

$^{1}/_{2}$ cup finely chopped radishes

1 tablespoon fresh tarragon leaves or $^{1}/_{2}$ teaspoon dried, crumbled

salt and freshly ground pepper to taste

In a skillet or sauté pan over moderately high heat, bring the oil to rippling. Add the vinegar, peas, scallions, radishes, and tarragon leaves. Stir for 1 or 2 minutes or until just heated through and fragrant, season with salt and pepper, and serve.

Summer White Bean, Red Radish, Cucumber, Scallion, and Sour Cream Salad

When we were kids, we eagerly awaited the first appearance of red radishes, cucumbers, and scallions together at the greengrocer. Chopped and tossed with sour cream and loads of freshly ground black pepper and a heavy dose of salt, these vegetables truly marked the beginning of our summer. Now, because we love beans, we've added them for a soft texture to go with the crispy-crunchiness of the garden vegetables. Sometimes we add diced red bell peppers to the mix as well. At other times we use plain low-fat or nonfat yogurt instead of rich, wonderful sour cream.

Just before serving, toss all the ingredients together in a bowl. Or combine the prepared vegetables in a bowl and serve with the sour cream passed separately. Diners can salt and pepper to taste.

Note: This salad can be served as a first course for 8. It also makes a perfect quick summer lunch or supper main dish accompanied by good Russian black bread.

1 small bunch of crisp red radishes, washed and trimmed (about $1/2$ pound), thinly sliced or coarsely chopped (the chopped leaves can also be used)

2 Kirby cucumbers, cut into $1/4$-inch dice

6 scallions, both white and green parts, cut into $1/4$-inch slices

1 10-ounce can small cannellini, drained and rinsed

2 tablespoons snipped fresh dill

$1/2$ teaspoon freshly ground pepper or more to taste

$1/2$ teaspoon salt or to taste

2 cups sour cream

SANDWICHES, SAUCES, AND DESSERTS

Curried Pink Bean Puree with Herring on Pumpernickel

SERVES 4

In the Bastille district of Paris, where recently we lived for a few weeks, we saw many Parisians eating on the run. They'd walk down the street with half a baguette, split and filled with a slice of ham, the sandwich projecting from a neatly folded white paper bag. We noticed the same people eating the same sandwich day after day. How boring, we thought. Yet when we talked about it, we discovered that a tuna fish sandwich is to us what a ham sandwich is to a Parisian. Expedient. Sandwich fillings do take some thought. What can be quick and tasty, different from the usual deli fillings? The bread a change from white or whole-wheat toast? Here's one that started out as an hors d'oeuvre spread and blossomed into a full-fledged sandwich filling.

½ cup drained bottled herring fillets in wine sauce

1 10-ounce can pink beans, drained and rinsed

2 tablespoons minced red onion

2 tablespoons minced scallion greens

¼ cup homemade or good-quality bottled mayonnaise

½ teaspoon curry powder or to taste

½ teaspoon freshly ground pepper

2 tablespoons unsalted butter, softened (optional)

8 slices pumpernickel

4 romaine lettuce leaves

Chop the herring into ¼-inch pieces and pat dry with paper towels.

Puree the beans in a blender or food processor or mash well with a fork.

In a bowl, stir together the herring, bean puree, onion, scallion greens, mayonnaise, curry powder, and pepper. The mixture can be made a day in advance and kept covered and chilled.

Lightly butter 4 slices of the pumpernickel, spread some of the herring mixture on each, and top the filling with a lettuce leaf and a slice of the bread. Cut into thirds on the diagonal and serve.

Note: Sour cream can be substituted for the mayonnaise. Add 1 teaspoon of lemon juice to the mixture if you do.

White Bean, Anchovy, and Egg Salad Sandwiches on Black Bread

SERVES 6

Egg salad laced with anchovies is one of our favorite sandwich fillings. The beans, we discovered, not only stretch the filling but also add another texture and counteract some of the cholesterol by spreading 4 eggs over 6 servings. The vast amount of fiber in the beans also helps remove some of the cholesterol before it gets into the bloodstream.

1/4 cup homemade or good-quality bottled mayonnaise

1 2-ounce can flat anchovies, drained, patted dry, and minced

3 or 4 drops of Tabasco sauce

1 teaspoon ground cumin

1 tablespoon Dijon mustard

1 tablespoon fresh lemon juice or to taste

3 scallions, both white and green parts, chopped

1/2 teaspoon freshly ground pepper

1 15-ounce can small cannellini, drained and rinsed

4 hard-cooked eggs, finely chopped or grated

12 slices of black bread or pumpernickel

1 thinly sliced cucumber

In a bowl, stir together the mayonnaise, anchovies, Tabasco, cumin, Dijon, lemon juice, scallions, and pepper. Stir in the beans and eggs and add more mayonnaise if necessary.

Spread on 6 slices of black bread, arrange slices of cucumber over the egg salad filling, and top with the remaining slices of bread.

Cut each sandwich in half on the diagonal and serve.

White Bean and Garlic Spread for Chicken Club Sandwiches on Brioche Toast

SERVES 4

Here we reinvent the club sandwich using the recipe for pureed white beans with garlic, along with fresh basil, to add a definite Mediterranean flavor to this quintessential American triple-decker concoction of grilled chicken and bacon. Seasoned bean purees make wonderful spreads for sandwiches all by themselves, layered thickly on the bread and topped with a slice of sweet onion, and are perfect bases for all kinds of sandwiches: cold cuts and smoked chicken or turkey or paired with grilled vegetables, melted cheese, fish, or seafood. They add texture, taste, moisture, and nutrition.

In a skillet over moderate heat, cook the bacon, turning it often, until it is crisp. Drain on paper towels.

Pour off all but 1 tablespoon of the fat from the skillet and add the chicken. Over moderate heat, sauté the chicken for 6 to 8 minutes on each side, or until just springy to the touch, and transfer it to a work surface or cutting board. Let the chicken cool for several minutes until it can be handled and cut it into thin slices.

Meanwhile, spread one side of each piece of toast with a layer of bean puree, sprinkle it with salt and pepper, and layer 4 of the toasts with a basil sprig, a tomato slice, an onion slice, and a bacon slice.

Top each sandwich with another slice of toast, bean puree side up, a basil sprig, a tomato slice, an onion slice, and one fourth of the chicken slices. Cover each sandwich with one of the remaining toasts, bean side down, pressing it firmly. Cut each sandwich in half, secure the halves with toothpicks, and serve.

4 slices lean bacon

1 whole skinless, boneless chicken breast (about $^1/_2$ pound), patted dry and seasoned well with freshly ground pepper

12 slices of brioche or other egg bread such as challah, lightly toasted

1 cup puree of white beans with roasted garlic and rosemary (page 58)

salt and freshly ground pepper to taste

8 fresh basil sprigs

8 thin ripe tomato slices

8 thin red onion or other sweet onion slices

Dilled Bean Puree
with Smoked Salmon on Pumpernickel

SERVES 4

After years of eating cream cheese and lox on a bagel, we had smoked salmon in Paris and Copenhagen on black bread spread with butter, and we were hooked. Of course, on the side were capers, lemon wedges, chopped onion, and dill sprigs. When we wanted a hearty smoked salmon sandwich for a seaside picnic and needed something to hold the capers, dill, and chopped onion so they wouldn't spill out from between the slices and end up in the sand, this invention was our solution—the hit of the picnic.

$\frac{1}{2}$ stick ($\frac{1}{4}$ cup) unsalted butter, softened

1 tablespoon fresh lemon juice

1 cup unseasoned white bean or chickpea puree

1 tablespoon drained bottled capers

1 tablespoon minced fresh dill

1 small red onion, finely chopped

1 teaspoon freshly ground pepper

8 slices of pumpernickel bread

$\frac{1}{2}$ pound thinly sliced smoked salmon

In a small bowl, cream together the butter, lemon juice, and bean puree. Add the capers, dill, onion, and pepper and stir until the mixture is well combined.

Spread the dilled bean puree on one side of each slice of bread. Layer half the puree-spread bread slices evenly with the salmon and top them with the remaining puree-spread bread slices, pressing them together firmly.

Cut the sandwiches in half diagonally and serve.

Note: This dilled bean puree also works with the smoked salmon (or with jarred salmon roe) as an hors d'oeuvre. Just spread the puree on triangles of thin cocktail pumpernickel, top with a sliver of smoked salmon (or several grains of salmon roe), garnish with a tiny frond of dill, and serve open-faced.

Try substituting thin rounds of daikon radish for the pumpernickel. Less filling, and the radish offers both a nice crunch and a little bite.

No-Cook Adzuki Bean, Parmesan, and Parsley Pasta Sauce

No cooking, no kidding. One nice thing about canned beans is that they're already cooked so they can be used for recipes like this pasta sauce, which is not necessary to heat. Just toss the creamy pink, fresh-tasting sauce with the hot pasta and enough of the hot cooking water to thin it a little. If you make the sauce ahead and chill it (it will keep in an airtight container for 3 days), just bring it to room temperature before using it. We leave some of the beans out of the pureeing process and add them to the sauce to give it some additional texture and eye appeal.

In a food processor, blend together about 1 cup of the beans, the Parmesan, parsley, garlic, and olive oil until the mixture is a coarse paste. Add the milk, salt, and pepper and process the sauce until it is combined well. Transfer the sauce to a bowl and fold in the remaining beans.

The sauce will keep chilled in an airtight container for 3 days. To serve, toss the room-temperature sauce with hot cooked pasta (we prefer shapes like shells, penne, or bow ties, but linguine, fettuccine, and thin spaghetti are fine) and enough of the cooking water to let it coat the pasta evenly.

1 15-ounce can adzuki beans, drained and rinsed

¾ cup freshly grated Parmesan

½ cup chopped fresh parsley leaves

1 large garlic clove, chopped

2 tablespoons olive oil

½ cup milk (either whole or 1% low-fat)

1 teaspoon salt or to taste

1 teaspoon freshly ground pepper

Chickpea Stuffing for Turkey

Traditionally Thanksgiving turkeys are filled with a chestnut stuffing. With packaged whole peeled chestnuts at a premium and peeling fresh ones from scratch one of the most time-consuming, tedious, and thankless kitchen tasks, we have come up with an admirable (and prettier) alternative: chickpeas. Chickpeas retain even more texture than chestnuts do in the finished baked stuffing, lend their own nutty flavor, and keep their pinky-beige color intact. If you have a favorite chestnut stuffing recipe that your family loves, by all means use it—just substitute chickpeas for the chestnuts (1 19-ounce can for 1 pound fresh chestnuts or ³/₄ pound vacuum-packed whole chestnuts). You won't fool anyone, and, perhaps, start a new tradition.

6 cups torn bite-size pieces of day-old homemade-style white bread or challah

1 stick (¹/₂ cup) unsalted butter

2 medium onions, chopped

4 celery ribs, chopped

3 tablespoons minced fresh sage leaves or 1 tablespoon dried, crumbled

2 tablespoons minced fresh thyme leaves or 2 teaspoons dried, crumbled

1 tablespoon minced fresh rosemary leaves or 1¹/₂ teaspoons dried, crumbled

1 tablespoon minced fresh savory leaves or 1 teaspoon dried, crumbled

1 teaspoon salt or to taste

1 teaspoon freshly ground pepper

1 19-ounce can chickpeas, drained and rinsed, left whole or crushed lightly with the back of a glass tumbler

¹/₂ cup finely chopped fresh parsley leaves

Preheat the oven to 325°.

In a shallow baking pan, spread the bread pieces in one layer, toast them in the oven, stirring occasionally, for 10 to 15 minutes or until they are golden, and transfer them to a large bowl.

Meanwhile, in a large skillet or sauté pan over moderately low heat, melt the butter. When the foam subsides, add the onions, celery, sage, thyme, rosemary, savory, salt, and pepper and cook, stirring, until the vegetables are softened, about 5 minutes. Add the chickpeas and cook the mixture, stirring, for 1 minute.

Add the vegetable/bean mixture to the bread pieces in the bowl, tossing the mixture well. Stir in the parsley and more salt and pepper to taste if desired and let the stuffing cool completely.

Note: To prevent bacterial growth, *do not stuff the turkey in advance,* especially not with hot stuffing.

This stuffing can be made one day in advance and kept covered and chilled.

Any excess stuffing can be packed into an oiled baking pan or heatproof casserole and set aside to be slipped into the oven to bake about 1 hour before the bird is done.

Pungent Black Bean and Garlic Sauce for Asparagus

MAKES ABOUT 1¼ CUPS. ENOUGH FOR 24 STALKS OF ASPARAGUS TO SERVE 4 TO 6

Fermented black beans can be found in any Asian or specialty food market. They're aromatic and sharp flavored and usually used sparingly (rinsed first to rid them of excess salt). This sauce is especially good with asparagus (cooked for 6 to 8 minutes, depending on their thickness), which, as far as we are concerned, is the signal that spring has arrived—but you might like to try it on green beans or broccoli. Another sign of spring is the appearance of soft-shell crabs, which also benefit from a coating of this tangy sauce, as do many other vegetables and shellfish.

1 tablespoon peanut oil

1 heaped tablespoon minced garlic

1 tablespoon grated or minced fresh peeled ginger

⅓ cup minced bottled pimiento or roasted red pepper

2 tablespoons fermented black beans, rinsed, drained, and lightly crushed

1½ tablespoons dry sherry

1 tablespoon soy sauce

pinch of sugar

1½ cups chicken broth

1 tablespoon cornstarch

1 tablespoon cold water

½ teaspoon freshly ground pepper

In a skillet or wok over moderately high heat, bring the oil to rippling. Add the garlic, ginger, and pimiento and stir-fry until the garlic barely turns golden, about 1 minute. Add the beans and stir-fry for 2 minutes more. Add the sherry and boil the mixture for 1 minute. Stir in the soy sauce, sugar, and broth, lower the heat to simmer, and cook the mixture, stirring occasionally, for 10 minutes.

In a small bowl, dissolve the cornstarch in the water, whisk it into the bean mixture, and continue to simmer the sauce until it is slightly thickened, about 2 minutes. Add the pepper, stir well, and serve the sauce over asparagus, steamed only until it is crisp-tender.

Tofu Mayonnaise

There is no substitute for real mayonnaise. However, there is an alternative for those who must cut down on egg consumption and want a more healthful, cholesterol-free dressing for potato, tuna, or other salads. Tofu mayonnaise is not traditional, not the same as the classic homemade egg and olive oil union or even the commercial bottled kind, but it's a wonderful compromise. Blend it to suit your own taste by changing the amount of mustard, lemon juice, salt, olive oil, or hot pepper sauce. Flavorings such as basil, garlic, horseradish, or herbs can also be added—depending on how you plan to use the mayonnaise. It's your call. Here is the basic formula:

In a blender or food processor, whirl all the ingredients until smooth and well combined (this is the time to add other flavorings if you like). If the dressing seems too thick, blend in about 1 tablespoon of cold water or more lemon juice. Transfer to a jar with a tight-fitting lid. Tofu mayonnaise will keep, refrigerated, for several weeks.

Note: The proportions remain the same to halve or double the yield.

10 ounces soft tofu (about 1 block)

¼ cup fresh lemon juice

2 teaspoons Dijon mustard or 1 teaspoon dry mustard

1 teaspoon salt or to taste

¼ cup light olive oil

1 teaspoon Tabasco or other hot pepper sauce

Adzuki Bean, Walnut, and Cocoa Meringues

MAKES ABOUT 2 DOZEN COOKIES

These chewy, chocolaty cookies are so quick to make that you can have them out of the oven and cool enough to eat in about 30 minutes. They may still be a little warm at that point, but so much the better. The nutty flavor of the beans supports the walnuts and chocolate creating a balance of sophisticated tastes and textures.

$2^1/_2$ cups confectioners' sugar

1 cup adzuki bean puree, made from 1 15-ounce can of adzuki beans, drained and rinsed—any excess saved for another use

1 cup walnuts, finely ground in a food processor or blender

7 tablespoons unsweetened cocoa powder

$^1/_8$ teaspoon salt

3 large egg whites, lightly beaten

$^1/_4$ teaspoon vanilla extract

1 teaspoon instant coffee powder

Preheat the oven to 350°.

In a large bowl, whisk together the confectioners' sugar, bean puree, walnuts, cocoa powder, salt, egg whites, vanilla, and coffee powder, stirring until the mixture is combined well.

Scoop up rounded tablespoons of the batter and put them on a parchment-lined baking sheet 2 inches apart, pressing them gently with a metal spatula to flatten them slightly. Bake the cookies in batches in the center of the oven for 15 to 18 minutes or until the tops appear dry and are lighter in color. Transfer them to racks to cool.

Store in an airtight tin or cookie jar until ready to serve. The cookies will stay chewy and moist for 2 or 3 days if stored properly.

Black Bean Chocolate Mousse Pie

MAKES 1 10-INCH PIE. SERVING 12

Using black bean puree (unseasoned, of course) in a dessert may seem unconventional, but it works brilliantly. Here it lends texture, taste, and color to the creation of a very elegant new sweet course, an intensely chocolaty chocolate mousse pie. The puree is incorporated into melted chocolate, then folded into the whipped cream so the filling is both rich and light. It's called a pie, but it actually looks more like a chocolate cheesecake. Very quick to make (it needs no baking), the pie does require refrigeration for at least 3 hours or overnight to set the filling and meld the flavors. For a stronger bittersweet chocolate flavor, substitute strong coffee for the water.

In a food processor, coarsely grind the walnuts, add the chocolate wafers, and finely grind the mixture. With the motor running, add the butter and liqueur. Press the mixture onto the bottom and halfway up the sides of a 10-inch springform pan.

In the top of a double boiler or in a metal bowl set over a pan of barely simmering water, melt the chocolate with the water, stirring until the mixture is smooth. Remove the top of the double boiler or bowl from the stove and mix the bean puree into the chocolate until well incorporated. Set aside.

In a chilled metal bowl, beat the cream until it holds stiff peaks and fold it into the reserved chocolate/bean mixture. Mound the mousse into the springform pan, smoothing the top. Chill for 3 hours or overnight.

Just before serving, remove the side of the pan, sieve the cocoa evenly over the top of the pie, and transfer it on its metal base to a cake dish.

½ cup walnut pieces

½ pound (about 32) chocolate wafers, broken into pieces

½ stick (¼ cup) unsalted butter, melted

2 tablespoons coffee liqueur (Kahlúa, Tia Maria, etc.) or rum

7 ounces best-quality bittersweet chocolate, chopped

¼ cup water

1 cup black bean puree, thinned with 2 tablespoons strong coffee

1½ cups heavy whipping cream, very cold

2 tablespoons unsweetened cocoa powder

Sweet and Spicy Bean Dessert Spread

MAKES ABOUT 2 CUPS

Here's a new way to serve cookies: with a sweet and spicy spread to slather on just as you would serve a cheese spread with crackers. Try it with vanilla wafers, shortbread, chocolate cookies, gingersnaps, or any other plain cookie you can dream up. Use the dessert spread to create sandwich cookies—a healthier answer to Oreos. Or you can serve it as you would a breakfast jam, to spread on toast, muffins, or croissants and surprise your family's taste buds first thing in the morning. Add more yogurt to thin it a little, and you have a dip for fresh fruit slices—dessert's answer to crudités. You'll probably think of dozens of other ways to use it once you taste it. As a filling for layer cake? Swirled into hot breakfast cereal? Thinned as a sauce for ice cream?

1 15-ounce can white beans, drained and rinsed

$^1/_4$ cup confectioners' sugar or more to taste

$^1/_2$ teaspoon freshly grated nutmeg

1 teaspoon ground cinnamon

$^1/_2$ teaspoon ground cardamom

$^1/_2$ cup dried currants, raisins, or banana chips

2 tablespoons nonfat plain yogurt

1 tablespoon fresh lemon juice or grated lemon zest

Whirl all the ingredients in a food processor until smooth and fragrant. Stop several times to scrape down the sides if necessary.

The spread keeps chilled in an airtight container for up to 2 weeks. Present it in a bowl or crock surrounded by your choice of one or more plain cookies.

INDEX